B... BOOK VERSION

O CHINADA

THE MANCHURIAN CANADIAN

COMMUNIST PATSY OF CANADA: CHANNELING CASTRO

by
RICHARD ABRAM ROSENBERGER

ISBN: 978-1-7775243-3-3

Cover by author

INKLETTER LTD. PUBLISHING

Any bulk or signature versions of this book are available for purchase upon request by email. For permission requests, write to the publisher "Attention Permissions Coordinator" at email address: info@ochinada.com.

Get "Behind the Scenes" Access to:

OCHINADA.COM

THE MANCHURIAN CANADIAN

Comment, challenge or contribute to the *ONLINE OPEN BOOK VERSION*.

Including access to all online media, updates, links, corrections and any archived material; with your free subscription request by email:

info@ochinada.com

DEDICATION

Canadian Patriots of

Freedom Convoy 2022

You defended your nation,

and inspired the world!

ACKNOWLEDGMENTS:

First, I want to remember those who gave their lives to defend our Canada. From First Nations to all Nations represented as natural-born or immigrant Canadians, who have founded our country and preserved it through many tragic and heartbreaking struggles. Many of them died in battle to preserve their way of life and honor their ancestor's sacrifice and labor. You invested more than life; you invested hope in faith that someday others would reap the benefits of your dreams. We owe you a debt we cannot pay because you paid a debt you did not owe. So, we pay our respect and honor to your legacy.

Second, I am grateful to **Freedom Convoy 2022** for taking the last bits of their livelihoods leftover from the Trudeau Communist Mandates and investing them into the heart and soul of Canada! Some of you paid the highest price to preserve our freedoms; you were an example of peace in the face of government terrorism. Some of you are still paying as a hostile treasonous dictatorship has illegally targeted you. Your demonstration will go down in history as a patriotic moment for Canada; you did your heroic ancestors proudly; you have inspired me and revived my love for Canada!

CONTENTS

Dedication 3
Acknowledgments: 5
Introduction 9
Author's Notes 10
Blog Burning 11
Manchurian Candidate 15
Manchurian Blood Pact 25
Manchurian Plague 2.0 33
Manchurian Media 39
Manchurian Model 49
Manchurian Global 57
Manchurian Dream 67
The Manchurian Canadian 81
Marx Of The Beast 87
Don't Call Them Liberals 95
Western Communists 103

The Grave Reset 111

World Economic Führer 119

Globalist Citizen 125

Civil Destruction 135

Socialist Justice Warrior 141

Who's Your Daddy? 151

Love of God and Country 159

The Ties That Blind 169

Reflection On Reflection 177

O Chinada 185

Cold-Weather Friend 193

Channeling Castro 199

Magna Carta 207

The Patsy 217

Autocoup 227

Just a Thought 235

Conclusions 239

INTRODUCTION

'OCHINADA: THE MANCHURIAN CANADIAN' is a *BLOG2BOOK VERSION*, written in a blog-style with references and quotes interlaced within the body of the text. Bible quotes are from The Authorized King James Version (KJV) and incorporate personal paraphrasing of the text. For dramatization and clarity, each opinion, quote, and reference is captioned and emphasized with font size, **bold** or *italicized*. **Any** *implied* emphasis is mine alone, which may or may not be fair to any subject context. I encourage the reader to follow links to check each in their respective reference.

All personal references, assertions to the summary of facts, or conclusions **are my opinions only**. These are my understandings and thoughts on subjects that may or may not be established by authors quoted, sources cited, and information deduced to form my thesis. All online links were available and active for follow-up at the time of publication; broken links after this production cannot be corrected herein; I intend to provide an online site **OCHINADA.COM** to post corrections, deletions, clarifications, and reviews.

AUTHOR'S NOTES

This is where the author introduces themselves with their excellent educational creds or some self-deprecating remarks. If I could have, trust me, I would have remained anonymous as in my blog for many years. But at this point, that is not an option.

Too many good souls have had private information doxed, their reputations slandered, and their livelihoods destroyed, all because they fought tyrannical despots for the freedom of Canada. In the face of such patriotism, I cannot keep silent.

I am just a small-town working-class *guy* with experience in farming, oil field, construction, trucking, retail grocery, and business. I hold a *Ph.D.* at the ***School of Hard Knocks*** and a *B.A. in* ***Survival,*** made possible by years of humbling circumstances.

I have helped with two youth outreach centers that lasted a few years, worked as a volunteer minister, and published my first book in 2020. I love my beautiful wife and am so proud of my children.

I went to school with a guy named Guy; my favorite hockey player's name was Guy. And I have found that I am no more important than the ***next guy*** or the ***last guy***. My name is Richard, but I can be a real "Dick" (if only I were American)!

BLOG BURNING

Today's fascists aren't burning books... **they are burning blogs!** By "shadow banning" and filtering out certain profiles, the *China-style* social credit gets applied throughout our media posts. We aren't simply censored; we are canceled if not in lockstep with Globalists.

In honor of those keyboard warriors who have sacrificed much to plead their case to end up with spit in their face, I plead mine. Many need to know where a person can get links, videos, and media from top scientists and front-line workers, but they cannot find this life-saving information **because it gets taken down by blog burners!**

Canada has a history of brutal attacks against personal freedom... *"for the greater good,"* ...**but whose greater good?** I offer my voice to help millions of hands-on workers, manufacturers, truckers, oil field workers, cooks, servers, the retail workforce, and millions of others not represented. These keep our nation operational when not being interrupted by political menace. Such *poly-ticks* pit one group of Canadians against another to create chaos and then offer solutions that we would naturally enjoy without their obstruction.

There is no possible way to include or address all these offenses levied against our rights in one book. Many books are doing justice, but where can we find them? **As each moment clicks along, many heroic daily-life stories get told, but who will hear them?** The Old Testament of the Bible has a gem of insight and inspiration for such a time...

> "And the LORD answered me, and said, Write the vision, and make it plain upon tablets, so that he who reads may run with it."
>
> — Habakkuk 2:2

These written stories are intended to be read and understood well enough that the reader can "run with it." To learn and act on them! But instead, these stories, labors, love, and struggles are lost to the control of a **handful of overlords** who would kill thought and will, keeping the masses engaged in **State-controlled** media and medical mandates.

This *"OPEN BOOK"* links to online free thought and free dissemination of information for those inquiring minds still seeking. One can go directly to the source and find a live account free from the filters and credit-score censorship. Another *side of the coin* would be to provide a **"KEEPSAKE"** book for those wanting to remember *better days of Canada*, her rights, and her freedoms before they get stripped from ***our cold dead fingers.***

OCHINADA.COM will provide a space for Canadians to share their experiences freely and a whistleblower's forum to get their voices heard. And this paper copy as an "old-school" life hack to bypass the social media mob... like a billboard on life's highway, we want to provide a memorable physical example of Canadian free speech.

This book is for the everyday parent, inquiring student, and ordinary Canadian corralled by unconstitutional mandates. This book is for the voiceless millions trampled on by *horses* of an oppressive Canadian Government. And for the loud, proud freedom founders, as they refuse to go down without a fight. From convoys to street protests, shoppers without masks, to businesses without "the pass," ...we uphold that patriotic torch handed to us by those at rest under the turf.

Be it known to the fascist foe; that we will not break trust with those who sleep, though poppies grow—

" Take up our quarrel with the foe!
To you from failing hands we throw
The torch; be yours to hold it high!
If ye break faith with us who die
We shall not sleep, though poppies grow
In Flanders fields."

There is only one passion that I hold dearer to me than my Canadian citizenship, and that is my Heavenly citizenship. I love my country, but I would be lost to a mere existence here and now without my love of God and the hope in my final destiny beyond that turf. Like the billions who find their hope beyond the grave, we are inspired past the fear one can face here and now to make life count!

In my youth, I laughed at the thought of patriotism, but no longer. Without hope beyond the death threatened upon us, one can only succumb to Marxist threats and fake promises! My love of God and country has been revived from Remembrance Days' inspiration and walks among the gravestones of my passed loved ones. **Will I meet them in glory or in cowardice?**

I desire to complete my book and publish my take on this move against our nation, but I cannot do it without your experiences and testimony. **This book aims to reward the patriot and expose the traitor**; we have worked too hard and endured too much to dissolve our nation into a new global colonial slave-state. It took me some 40 years to write my first book *GARGANTUOUS*, but I **don't** think we have another 40 to finish at that rate. At worst, this attempt falls on the trash heap of censored thought. I appeal to fellow citizens of Canada, those still free enough to have their voices heard; let it not be said that we merely stood by.

MANCHURIAN CANDIDATE

The Manchurian Candidate by Richard Condon is a political thriller first published in 1959, having two film adaptations, one in 1962 (with Frank Sinatra) and the other in 2004 (with Denzel Washington). It's a story about soldiers taken as prisoners and brainwashed by the communists to become sleeper agents in America. As the plot goes, these agents find themselves unraveling due to the immense psychological pressures as their realities blend with implanted memories, revealing the shocking truth that they have committed atrocities against their patriotic oaths and allegiances.

Closer to home than that, **the mother of the prominent traitor had been in bed *politically* with the same Communists** seeking to destroy America!

It is laughable to think that a plot to brainwash a few good men would even be needed to take out an American President when it seems this Biden is as corrupt as they come and would happily do their bidding without the brainwashing! Like all the conflicts of interest of Joe Biden, his son Hunter gets to oversee billions from China. And with all the evidence of payoffs and bribes, corruption doesn't look like it is merely a family affair but rather a sanctioned art by America's top 3-letter agencies!

Who needs secretly brainwashed chumps when blatant audacious in-your-face corruption goes unchecked?

How do these creatures of greed and deception operate with such impunity? Most people believe the best about their fellow countrymen and are unwilling to think that people can be such liars, cheats, sociopaths, or just greedy bastards!

Regardless of how often we read the history of governments feeding their people to famines, flames, and child-labored slavery, the millions of deaths often go unregistered in our carefully washed brains! Many cannot wrap their heads around the apparent fact that some would sell out their grandmothers to get ahead. So, consequently, selling out their birthright "for the greater globalist good" is just a proverbial walk in the park!

Somehow it is the foreign Communist that is evil, depending on how much Hollywood you follow. But the foreign Communist only exposes the *Western Devil*, just after these Marxists wipe their bloodied hands on the capitalism that fueled their so-called Socialism. The difference is that profits in Capitalism are produced by voluntary investment and personal sacrifice. In contrast, earnings in Communist nations are commanded at the end of a gun or social(ist) credit enslavement, corporate thievery, and espionage.

The *Manchurian Candidate* conspiracy is merely a ruse to deflect the attention of patriots as they call out the... ***"evil few"*** ...while ignoring the corrupt globalist masses **within** the rank and file!

As long as people believe the adage of ***"a few bad apples,"*** they will never discover the sorry truth that an entire generation cannot distinguish an "apple" from an "orange!" When it comes to right and wrong, they have been conditioned from their youth in school to reject the very notion of morality for more relative terms.

When *THEY* tell you that *"you will own nothing and be happy," THEY* neglected to inform you *THEY* redefined "happiness." The kind of *happiness* in Communist nations forces their children into sweat-shops, daughters off to bitter prostitution, and parents for re-education! IT isn't "genocide" just avoiding "climate change." We don't call it stealing everyone's goods... we just call it: "The Great RESET!"

Our Founding Fathers knew what tyranny looked like and gladly laid down their lives to protect their children's future from such fascists. But that is the **same kind of future their children now embrace** and don't know what awaits them. As long as they obey and agree to promote the Globalist agenda, Socialist Media won't cancel them!

There is equality among those who will own nothing, but it will not be happy! The love of God and Country that fueled our Founding Fathers; is now extinguished by Communist reeducation. The standard for patriotic "normalcy" is pulled down like a statue from a withered past, only to be replaced by cardboard cut-outs of woke virtue-signaling puppets spewing mantras of Marx.

Is this the *Zombie* apocalypse? Yes!
Sadly, they are already dead but just don't know it.

For one to believe the promises of Carl Marx is to be ignorant of history. Why is only a mere skeletal framework of history taught in school and not the very study of ideologies that caused such death and destruction? Because, if such a comparison of Capitalism vs. Socialism were had, one would discover that Capitalism has lifted more people out of poverty than anything else! The free enterprise system brought the likes of the wealthiest people on the planet to such heights from their meager beginnings. Such Capitalism they no longer want because it runs a risk of competing with their monopolies under pseudo-socialism and the final communist wealth transfer to their pockets.

I admit that the best form of free enterprise is Capitalism with actual Socialism tendencies —a capitalism where free enterprise is unhindered, uncoerced, and unmanipulated by monopolies controlling the markets. A Capitalism where taxing is fair and unavoidable without the loopholes, and such proceeds get held to account and not mere slush funds of politicians. A Capitalism where those seeking to off-shore their profits and drain the nations that provided such wealth and prosperity; will face tariffs or heavy taxation. Without hedge funds and those who would influence not only stocks but the very *futures* of a nation!

Such Capitalism is yet to be enjoyed **...and yet, still healthier than Communism on its best day.**

One might say the same about Socialism and how it has yet to be realized under its fundamental ideals, where everyone can share wealth and prosperity equally. But this kind of Socialism is predicated on a world with a work ethic and the absence of greed. This format gets fueled by the wanting of what another person has and the empowering of an unaccountable government to confiscate said goods for distribution among the "less fortunate."

The confiscation of goods is easy, but the riddance of the greed within those who would commit such acts, not so much! Anyone comfortable with that kind of theft would also be pleased with tyrannical, murderous lies and deceit.

Did you ever notice how those heads of State in Communist/Socialist countries live so lavishly on the backs of those at the bottom in such desolate, impoverished squalor? Did you see how many of those heads of State in Capitalist free enterprise nations have come from such meager beginnings and now command such wealth and prosperity?

We know some failures in Capitalism exist today because we see the **degradation of the laws** that keep such in check. We are witnessing the Marxist infiltration into the system that provides the very law and order to see the success of Capitalism and free enterprise. Marxism thrives on chaos, anarchy, and the lawless unraveling of society so that they can step in and "save the day" with more control and fewer freedoms.

Not realized is that **Marxism is merely a ruse for Monarchy**. Marxism promises fair play and equity for the oppressed and destroys a society built on merit and a fair market. What follows is the breakdown of the very fabric of civil existence, which is necessary for their enacting martial law and total government *intervention*.

The pattern is easily repeatable: create a crisis so big that only *THEY* alone can save the poor people from! Create a volatile chaotic murderous mayhem so widespread that only they can (by military force) bring it under control. The kind of control the average person will be begging for and an authoritarian government eager to provide!

And this is the model that will return nations and the very Globe to a Feudal Monarchy. China has already returned to an emperorship under leader Xi Jinping. **Yet *"his lands"* are merely holdings that he can control only under a *Globalist Monarchy*** that employs his services, military force, and manufacturing.

Soon all nations will be sectioned into kingdoms under their "kings" to pay respect, offerings, and allegiance to a One World Order Monarchy. A one-world Dictator offering *"realms of glory"* to those who would sell out their national security for globalist citizenship and *feudal lordship* of their lands. If you want to know who holds such position and power globally, look no further than the one who controls the money and landmass.

Don't look at the world's Billionaires as independent because of their wealth. Instead, their wealth depends on a system that defines the value of each dollar they own or own them! **Each dollar they have is indebted to a system that grants it a monetary value;** if that value ceases, so does their wealth. Their money is actual debt to a system they have a greater vested interest in keeping afloat!

This global monetary system supports such "financially independent" individuals under their control; **they don't have the freedom you might think.** They can only operate within the parameters offered to them inside such a system... they won't be your savior!

"The Great Reset" security offered to the world in exchange for their "independence" is a final wealth transfer (theft) by those who will dissolve the very hope of independent Nations, their citizenship, and their lands. All property and money will become the property of "Earth." Those non-elected few will rule the Earth in a *"New World Order"* that will bring ***"order"*** **to the CHAOS they are about to unleash on the world.**

Subsequently, all nations will be begging for relief from its fallout! People will get restricted to their "quarters" or regions and forbidden to travel with a livelihood based upon their "socialist credit" score or lack thereof. People have always traded independence for "security."

Klaus Schwab: World "Never" to return to normal:

> "Many of us are pondering when things will return to normal," writes Schwab. "The short response is: never." **—Paul Joseph Watson**, November 10, 2020

https://summit.news/2020/11/10/globalist-klaus-schwab-world-will-never-return-to-normal-after-covid

Big Pharma, Big Money, and Big Media are all in cahoots to reveal their ***villain*** of the Covid narrative: **it is the non-compliant!**

One doesn't need some secret fraternity to conjure up traitors against their nations, to hand it over to a cabal of Communist operatives. All that is necessary is to openly control people's minds through fear (real or imagined) against something that only the Global Government can fix. This sort of mind-control has never been globally possible until now. Now, this war for the soul of our nation is currently being played out before sleepy eyes!

As in the story of the Manchurian Candidate, "Major Bennett" **couldn't trust his *lying eyes*** and memories because he was conditioned to accept the alternative reality provided by his handlers.

As with ***St. Fauci***, patron saint of murderous medical mad science, having helped to either cook up the bug or finance the same lab that released this viral bio-weapon. He provided the USA with the worst advice on protecting and treating the infection (though he wrote papers on effective prophylactics). And is still employed and further celebrated even though he appears to be a modern Holocaust Criminal! We are conditioned to accept an alternative reality, where perpetrators of crimes against humanity are presented as *saviors*.

Thanks to Western *Journalism* and Mainstream News Media, the brainwashing is complete! **Fauci** may go down as the person who threw the WORST opening pitch of the season... instead of the person who may have been responsible for the most deaths around the Globe in the worst hostile fakeover of America! Like **Andrew Cuomo** being (socially) hung for some sexual harassment while commanding the Covid-deaths in seniors' homes!

The problem is that people cannot believe **their own eyes for the life of them** ...or consequently for the death of them.

MANCHURIAN BLOOD PACT

Along with most Westerners thinking —that people are *basically good* and that there are only "a few bad apples;" we believe other nations are like us and have enjoyed the kinds of freedom we have. The problem with that thinking is that some would like the *West* to fail badly because they see how we live in such security and potential while they have had to claw for every meal.

Theirs is not mutual respect and love for culture; their pain has forged them into a determined lot that will no longer be taken advantage of! Do not think it is with pride that they have had to *sell their children* into slavery to make our shoes, phones, and clothes! Rather sorrowing patience! Once they gain the very leverage and power to turn the tables, you can be sure they will; then WE will serve them; WE will be their reserves, resources, and commodities!

You can be sure there won't be any "diplomacy" when they become the world powers. If we doubt that for a moment, we should dust off our history books that reveal deep-rooted blood pacts that propelled their nations to survival when they faced almost certain death. Did we tend to their wounds when they were under siege? Did we send aid when they were starving to death? Do we even care when their children are forced as slaves for Western wastefulness? Hardly! AND it will be with similar silence when it's our turn.

Some 100 years ago, under the support of 85 percent of an impoverished China, Mao Zedong formed the Chinese Communist Party from a 70-year-old Marxist Communist Manifesto published in 1848 by Karl Marx and Friedrich Engels. **The Communist Manifesto** was to cause rioting by the *common* people to destroy the "upper class," freeing the lower class from governmental tyranny. It was a tyranny that would only change hands to become worse than its predecessors, as an estimated 65 million Chinese died due to Mao's "socialist" China.

To celebrate this legacy, Xi Jinping (channeling) Mao Zedong addressed the world with a threat that **anyone who came against China would have their heads "bashed" and "bloodied!"**

In the Manifesto, Communism has ten essential "planks" (more in chapter ***Marx of the Beast***)...

- Abolish Private Property and Public Land
- A Burdensome Progressive Income Tax.
- The Abolition of all Rights of Inheritance.
- Property Confiscation of Rebellious/ Immigrants.
- A State Central Bank Monopoly
- State Communication and Transportation.

- State Manufacturing, Farming, and Production.
- State Labor control, especially for Agriculture.
- State Farms and regional corporate planning.
- State Education with Industrial Production.

The Communist Manifesto is State oppression of the lower class and the impoverished because it confiscates their goods, workforce, inheritance, and freedoms while controlling their education and social structure! Though it promises the abolition of the "upper class," one can see how China's leaders live in stark hypocrisy to an equality with those enslaved by their tyrannical policies.

Also, Communism isn't satisfied with mere economic and political reform; it seeks to replace Religion and its moral ideals with State-worship and complete obedience instead of Christianity's soul-freeing tenants. Marxism, as applied, is totalitarian oppression and political hypocrisy.

Exactly 90 years ago, Joseph Stalin started the liberation of China via Manchuria through a self-serving move against the growing threat of an invading Japanese military. It secured a Stalinist Marxist blood-pact forever with China and Russia. Now it is an unstoppable force that will realize the Great Global Reset!

Today we see an inseparable Vladimir Putin and Xi Jinping in a blossoming bromance, a marriage prearranged a century ago. Xi Jinping appears to incorporate the most effective traits of Stalin's *"repression of workers"* and Marx's "*elevation of workers"* ideology of State-controlled workers and the repression of rebellious free-thinkers! Both Mao and Stalin would have been proud of him.

> "Why 'best friends' Vladimir Putin and Xi Jinping's bromance is blossoming ...China's president has called Putin his "best and bosom friend". And on their many meetings the pair have exchanged gifts, including pandas, ice cream and jewelery." **—The Sun**: http://www.thesun.co.uk
> https://www.youtube.com/watch?v=rnKb0mR5ZU4

> "Why China's Love for Putin Is Dangerous ...even though Russia and China were once ideological enemies that even met in battle, **common Marxist roots** and a historical fraternal alliance still form a foundation for today's amicable relations."**—David Gitter** August 06, 2014
> https://thediplomat.com/2014/08/why-chinas-love-for-putin-is-dangerous/

Without the Stalinist intervention in Manchuria, China may have been under Japanese control even today! There is such an underlying Chinese disdain for Japan and the USA partnership. While the USA was perceived to have kicked China to the curb, the Soviet Socialist Republics (USSR) was viewed as its savior by defeating advances by Japan to conquer China. And since the USA has always been rivals with China, it makes sense logistically, politically, and historically that a China/Russia alliance sees the end of America as the dominant Global Power.

> "America's dominance is over. By 2030, we'll have a handful of global powers" —**Robert Muggah** November 11, 2016, | World Economic Forum

Could it be that by the 100th anniversary of the USSR's delivery of China from the invasion of Japan, we will see a China/Russia Global Dominance, both financially and militarily? Who will stop it? Will Joe Biden? He is the one who is seen as currently taking bribes from China, and his son Hunter is in control of billions from China! Traitors also rule America!

That Democrat administration is doing everything possible to dismantle America with help, or more accurately, by directing its corrupt 3-letter agencies that have officially merged with the New World Order Globalist Super Powers! The China/Russia alliance is also a front for those financing this **"New and Ambitious"** work with the Queen of England (more later).

Let it suffice to say that after America is dismantled by **fraudulent elections** or destroyed financially by lockdowns, the Communist infiltration will be complete. The World Bank Financing of China will have *paid off* more than one could imagine—in the transfer of wealth and private property confiscated in this **III World (COVID) War**. I MIGHT ADD THAT this *III World (COVID) War* will be won without a *shot*... **unless you count vaccines!**

A (low-grade) bio-weapon dropped by China will net an unfathomable return in more severe Covid case lockdowns, sickness, and weakening of the American Military and all governmental agencies; under more forced mandated vaccinations.

As America succumbs to the fear and disaffects of citizens while letting a Globalist Media Agenda off the hook for its participation, it will go the way of Canada and Australia—**part of the Queen's "private estate."** The Queen owns about 80%

of Canada and 23% of Australia as her "private estate." And in 2015, a **"New and Ambitious" treaty** between the Queen and China was made at Buckingham Palace...

> "Mr. President, Prince Philip and I are delighted to welcome you and Madame Peng to Buckingham Palace this evening. Your visit to the United Kingdom marks a milestone in this unprecedented year of co-operation and friendship between the United Kingdom and China, as we celebrate the ties between our two countries and prepare to take them to ambitious new heights... Yet it was China's desire to shape a new future which captivated us the most." —CGTN
> https://www.youtube.com/watch?v=QbC-LMHwRyE

IT seems the WEST is the LAST to know of the rallying of Globalist interests against their so-called "Independence."

North American occupants go about their busy COVID preoccupation, while the "powers that be" seem to have moved on to greater works and ventures as they prepare for the dismantling and the divvying up of America when the civil unrest fallout reaches its designed chaotic event. Eventually absorbed into a "Global Village," each peasant will be marked for value. Then the Globalists will provide their antidote for the poison they enforced, fueled by fear and the breakdown of society; the 'UN' will be the UNdoing of all national borders, identities, and constitutions protecting the rights of individuals.

> "Should Russian ground vehicles somehow be supported by China's massive, technologically advanced and fast-growing Navy, any advance could be nearly impossible to stop... **China's Navy, for example, is already larger than the U.S. Navy in terms of sheer numbers."** —The Frontier Post
> https://thefrontierpost.com/russia-and-china-strengthen-joint-military-to-military-exercises-express-mutual-trust/

A famous saying about strong family ties is, **"Blood is thicker than water."** Yet many do not know the full quote means something different than supposed. The complete rendering is, **"The blood of the covenant is thicker than the water of the womb,"** meaning blood spilled on battlefields makes bonds between soldiers stronger than family ties, **like China and Russia's blood pact!**

MANCHURIAN PLAGUE 2.0

Either the 7 Heads over the ***Dragon-Serpent Beast*** of China didn't get the memo or are about to make exception to ***The Art of War* for the West!** The "Seven Heads" I am referring to are the 7 Heads of China's Government; 1) Xi Jinping, 2) Li Keqiang, 3) Li Zhanshu, 4) Wang Yang, 5) Wang Huning, 6) Zhao Leji, 7) Han Zheng... and possibly their opportunity to give *"Sick Man" of* the West a little bit of their "own medicine!"

To appreciate the references for **"Manchurian Plague"** and **"Sick Man,"** one can look to the historical account of an ironically similar repetition of history that seems manufactured and far beyond coincidence. An excellent article to get a historical context of this chapter would be the following:

> "**The Manchurian Plague and COVID-19: China, the United States, and the "Sick Man," Then and Now** - In 1911, this weakened China faced an outbreak of pneumonic plague in Manchuria that killed more than 60 000 people. After the 1911 plague, a revolutionized China radically restructured its approach to public health to eliminate

> the stigma of being "the Sick Man." Ironically, given the US mishandling of the COVID pandemic, **observers in today's China are now calling the United States "the Sick Man of the West"**: a country burdened by opioid addiction, infectious disease, and an ineffective government. The historical significance of the phrase "Sick Man"—and its potential to now be associated with the United States..."
> —Ruth Rogaski PhD,
> https://ajph.aphapublications.org/doi/full/10.2105/AJPH.2020.305960

It has been said, *"Revenge is a Dish Best Served Cold"* —with the idea that revenge is more satisfying when one has had time to prepare it, being well-planned, long-feared, or unexpected!

WHAT IF your nation was deeply wounded by a plague that swept through unstoppable, killing virtually everyone who contracted it. Then the world kicked your country when it was down and helpless to survive such devastation; at a time, your citizens were already battling addiction, depression, and national financial ruin. Referring to your glorious homeland as *"the Sick Man of the Far East,"* your nation had the "opportunity" to turn the tables by *manufacturing* a crisis that would give ultimate revenge? **What if that's happening now?**

Well, the ***Revenge Theory*** of the *"Sick Man of the West/World"* goes something like...

1) Turn the USA into a nation of opiate addicts; **2)** Turn loose a bio-weapon into the world that would weaken the whole world, especially its economic powerhouse in the USA; **3)** Use Government Psychological Operations PSYOPS to cause confusion and division in the USA; **4)** China Assumes Global Leadership vicariously through Biden and Trudeau;

1) USA Opiate Addiction

> "**How China flooded the U.S. with lethal fentanyl, fueling the opioid crisis**" **—Adriana Belmont**
> https://finance.yahoo.com/news/chinas-role-in-the-us-fentanyl-epidemic-152338423.html

2) Bio-Weapon Infectious Disease

> **"It comes from the lab — the lab in Wuhan and the lab is controlled by China's government."**
> https://www.youtube.com/watch?v=7Lq3_rsBJ9w | https://nypost.com/2020/09/11/chinese-virologist-says-she-has-proof-covid-19-was-made-in-wuhan-lab

"**Canadian scientist sent deadly viruses to Wuhan lab**" —Karen Pauls
https://www.msn.com/en-ca/news/canada/canadian-scientist-sent-deadly-viruses-to-wuhan-lab-months-before-rcmp-asked-to-investigate/ar-BB15sidO

3) Gov Psychological Operations PSYOPS

"**Anthony Fauci:** No, right now people should not.. there is no reason for them to be walking around with a mask. When you're in the middle of an outbreak, wearing a mask might make people feel a little bit better and it might even block a droplet, but it's not providing the perfect protection that people think that it is."
—Edmund DeMarche | Fox News
https://www.foxnews.com/health/faucis-controversial-60-minutes-interview-about-mask-wearing-was-one-year-ago

Wait just a minute! **How is Anthony Fauci somehow some kind of *lab-coat* of China?** Surely, he cannot be responsible for the ineffective, mixed messaging on masks, vaccines, and actual COVID numbers? And yet there are scads of articles linking Fauci to China, and here is a couple:

"Documents show that the Wuhan Institute of Virology used a $3.7 million grant from the U.S. government to conduct coronavirus studies on mammals captured more than

1,000 miles away in Yunnan, according to the Daily Mail in April 2020."—Anne Walker https://m.thebl.tv/health/judicial-watch-sues-against-hhs-people-have-to-know-about-faucis-involvement-with-wuhan-institute.html

"Report: Dr. Fauci Helped Create The Corona Virus In China" —**Jim Clayton**, https://www.conservativedailynews.com/2020/11/report-dr-fauci-helped-create-the-corona-virus-in-china/

4) Vicarious Global Leadership

"Joe Biden once 'joked' about **China helping him become president**" —Jon Levine, New York Post, https://nypost.com/2020/09/05/joe-biden-once-joked-about-china-helping-him-become-president/

"Vice President Biden Speaks at the U.S.-China Strategic and Economic Dialogue - "I congratulated him on his elevation, I asked if he could possibly help me" https://www.youtube.com/watch?v=182NfOr6s-c

"Report: Hunter Biden's Connected to **'Chief Spy of China'** Through His Chinese-American Secretary ...It determined that the **millions of dollars transferred from the firm to Hunter and his uncle** "raise criminal financial,

counterintelligence and extortion concerns." —Edwin Mora, BREITBART
https://www.breitbart.com/politics/2021/05/07/report-hunter-bidens-connected-to-chief-spy-of-china-through-his-chinese-american-secretary/

"COVID Coverup: **Trudeau gov't helped China hide origins of COVID-19**"
—Keean Bexte, Rebel News
https://www.rebelnews.com/covid_coverup_trudeau_govt_helped_china_hide_origins_of_covid_19
https://www.youtube.com/watch?v=hYJL2Cn_9IY

"INTERNATIONALCOMMENTARY - **Chinese Leadership Corrupts Another UN Organization**" —Brett Schaefer / Dean Cheng / Klon Kitchen / May 11, 2020
https://www.dailysignal.com/2020/05/11/chinese-leadership-corrupts-another-un-organization/

Klaus Schwab says, **"we penetrate the cabinets."** A Marxist ***penetration*** of all levels of government has made it possible for a global **"Reset"** to be hatched from releasing a bioweapon plandemic, all while having experimental gene therapy vaccines with endless boosters ready to *treat* this manufactured chaos.

It could now be said...
'Revenge is a ***(Petri) Dish*** Best Served Cold!'

MANCHURIAN MEDIA

"In war, the way is to avoid what is strong and to strike at what is weak." —Sun Tzu

That sounds like the attack strategy of a hyena! "Attack the weak, and avoid the strong," a strategy that didn't work out so well for **Goliath!** Gone are the days of champion against champion, but if you call a war on the weak a "victory," you are following the wrong General.

Speaking of "GIANTS," get a look at these:

6 Media Companies who almost OWN IT ALL
https://www.webfx.com/blog/internet/the-6-companies-that-own-almost-all-media-infographic/

24 News Companies with Global control
https://vizworld.com/2019/12/24-companies-that-own-the-news-around-the-world-infographic/

32 Richest Media Moguls in The World
https://ceoworld.biz/2019/11/11/media-billionaires-richest-media-moguls-in-the-world-2019/

Here is how just 25 Corporations control ALL WORLD - Banking, Media, Food & Beverage, and Oil
https://internationalbusinessguide.org/corporations/

With only 25 Social Media platforms globally, it is apparent that our digest and progress are easily controlled by a couple of dozen heads that could easily fit a Global *roundtable*. Yet, not a roundtable for decision, that is left up to only two *companies*... Blackrock and Vanguard.

One might reference a favored media or two that seems to "stand alone" against the "bias" projected in 99% of what they see and hear; but how can we be sure that such contention isn't merely a focus on programmed or controlled "opposition" in the guise of independent journalism? Remember, the World's richest 1% own 82% of its wealth!

> "The best way to control the opposition is to lead it ourselves."
> —Vladimir Lenin (1870-1924), Russian Communist Leader

> "A Rundown of Major U.S. Corporate Media's Business Ties to China - It seems a number of major US media outlets have financial ties to the Chinese Communist Party, and it shows in their coverage."
> —Chrissy Clark, May 4, 2020
> https://thefederalist.com/2020/05/04/has-china-compromised-every-major-mainstream-media-entity/

And what better way to "control the opposition" than to let them decry the abuses of authoritarian governments, treasonous politicians, and social media monopolies? **Then keep just shy of exposing mass voter fraud in the only free nation that can do anything about these massive influences controlling all aspects of our world.** Other countries get exposed for their fraudulent election Coups overthrowing democracy, but coming out and saying that would upset the sleeping citizen.

After all, it is called the "American Dream," and we wouldn't want to wake anyone up! If militant America has a "dream" that is being systematically reinvented by a global *plandemic*, what do you think is happening in passive Canada?

Somehow, we have been "boiled alive" only to snap to and realize we are already seen as a "Socialist Country!" We fail to recognize that we are a bit slow on the uptake, which means we are already under a Communist Dictatorship! We have voted in our Dictators that have aligned Canada with Globalists against our will and vote!

One day we were a Nation; now, we are a Globalist Member-State, indebted beyond sustainability to China, and at odds with our biggest trading partner, which will soon be in a similar situation with China under Biden. America seems at least to be under some illusion of "Independence" while

Canada (fully aware) appears willing to trade both "Queen and Country" for a Global Emperor!

Who will sound the alarm? I have said it before; the alarm was sounded some 20-30 years ago! We are witnessing the last drips of the sprinkler system on the flames that engulf the structure. So, who or what are those "sprinklers" that try to cool the *tongues* of those caught in the hellfire of Socialism? In my opinion, a few of them are being used to carry a Trojan payload that will seal the fate of any remaining resistance to this world net.

The final deception to bring about the One World Government is the technologically advanced "scientific" 9th Wonder. IF the *8th Wonder* is human structures comparable to the 7th Wonder of Creation, the *9th Wonder* will be no less than an artificial *intelligence* replacement for free thought.

Who is this "god" so wonderful to the humanist? What can replace the Creator and redefine "Creation" but the global acceptance and recognition of U.F.O.s ...not as Unidentified, but as Identified and defined: **Lucifer in our final conflict!**

When certain *News Outlets* that trash the misinformation of the Military-Industrial Complex also swallow hook-line-and-sinker their *security briefs* that name *"UFO" threats* to our world... a "Strong Delusion" is about to take hold of the world! It is too late for people who accept a beyond-science phenomenon, which scientific laws and your own two eyes refute.

Much like *pandemics* that drop our National Defense, share our National Security, and combine our National Interests. As they say, global threats, security, and interests outweigh *selfish* national concerns. Big Government doesn't want the real issues entrusted to the people in our nations but wants to have "global citizens" who vote for "liberal" *Communists* every time! Whether it is Climate Change, CO.V.ID, or U.F.O. ...the ***global citizenry*** is willing to give up all private property, monetary independence, and free thought to "save their Mother Earth."

WHO can argue with Corona Vaccination IDs, *Identified* Flying Objects, ***Climate Chains***, the Global News/Entertainment, and Social Media en masse? Or even electronic ballot results? Constantly they trash national pride and tell us we are unpatriotic if we don't go along with their Communist Manifesto!

> "Justin Trudeau accepts global citizenship award from Atlantic Council think tank" — *Staff* the Canadian Press
> https://globalnews.ca/news/3757737/justin-trudeau-global-citizenship-award/

The Global Media plus-1 doctor's force tells us to get vaccinated with a dangerous experimental "gene therapy vaccine." While countless videos of doctors effectively treating COVID with preventative therapeutics, more have been taken down by Google/YouTube, banned by Facebook, and "canceled" on Twitter.

In unison, the Mainstream Media barks the same lines and mantras to brainwash the public that Fauci knows best; these same "doctors of death" have allegedly developed, patented, and released these pandemics on an unsuspecting public! Even doctors and virologists who voice their concerns about COVID policies are demonized or dismissed.

> "The Great Barrington Declaration –
> As infectious disease epidemiologists and public health scientists we have grave concerns about the damaging physical and mental health impacts of the prevailing COVID-19 policies, and recommend an approach we call Focused Protection."
> —The Great Barrington Declaration
> https://gbdeclaration.org/

Bill Gates confessed to investing in vaccinations because they had a 20:1 return on Investment.

> "Bill Gates: My' best investment' turned $10 billion into $200 billion worth of economic

> benefit - Investing in global health organizations aimed at increasing access to vaccines created a 20-to-1 return in economic benefit, ... Bill Gates told CNBC "The Best Investment I've Ever Made,"https://www.cnbc.com/2019/01/23/bill-gates-turns-10-billion-into-200-billion-worth-of-economic-benefit.html . . . https://www.cnbc.com/video/2019/01/23/bill-gates-and-the-return-on-investment-in-vaccinations-davos.html

> "A team of international researchers, including from India, have found that the COVID-19 virus' contains a tiny chunk of DNA that matched the sequence **patented** by Moderna **three years before** the onset of the pandemic." https://weather.com/en-IN/india/coronavirus/news/2022-02-26-new-study-finds-covid-19-dna-linked-to-moderna-patent-filed-in

It is no wonder that Globalist "team players" have got together with those who have developed and *patented COVID*; they monopolize on the fears and ignorance of people lined up to get their shot!

> *25 Corporations (over their subsidiary corporations) control ALL WORLD - Banking, Media, Food & Beverage, and Oil* https://internationalbusinessguide.org/corporations

—each pushing for their cut of that 20:1 ROIC for their part in this COVID EXTRAVAGANZA! We haven't even scratched the surface of the role of Big Pharma and China in the development of first the vaccines and second the therapeutics to treat the auto-immune disorders that seem to follow!

There is no need for the CURE when life-long TREATMENT is so damn lucrative!

It is easier to get a sick person to give up their rights to get *free* health care, as long as you make sure they don't find out it was you all along that made them sick!

It is easier for you to offer protection from *"ANTIFA"* **as long as they don't find out that you sent them to burn down your businesses and attack your freedoms *in the name of justice!*** It is easier to get people to go along with all-out Communism **as long as you promise not to go door-to-door breaking their legs**, hauling their kids away, publicly shaming and canceling them, or making legal protests illegal!

This is not the repeat of the former Nazi takeover; this is bigger and more sinister; evil has bred prolifically, and now there is no place to run from its slithering spawn! When **two-thirds of the countries on Earth are Marxist Socialist/Communist** and are all driven by the China Belt & Road Initiative, these 25 Corporations controlling ALL WORLD - Banking, Media, Food & Beverage, and Oil; will take our sovereignty!

ANOTHER thing to remember is that the enemy wants to avoid WAR at all costs because why should the enemy fight if you are willing to give up so easily? I say make the enemy fight for everything that he wants to steal! Make the enemy pay dearly in blood, sweat, and tears for every brick, belt, and road! The whole "Art of War" is to win wars without fighting, **and they are.**

I am not a Global Citizen like Trudeau; I am a Canadian Citizen! **We elect our representatives to represent us, not rule over us!**

With their Globalist Agendas, aspirations, or Initiatives, our politicians sell us out and trade our futures on a Global Stock Exchange, which has us all of no more value than cattle or sheep! Our Constitution, Laws, and Rights prevent **us** as Canadians from doing such, and it would be nothing less than treasonous if we did! And if Trudeau wants to give up his national identity and citizenship, I say he has the freedom to do so for himself and his family, **but not for Canada!**

And the MEDIA! These Corporate Communists want to go through our clothing for loose change and pick our bodies clean of jewelry, just like

George Soros did for the Nazis! These Global *Jurassic* blood-sucking parasites are proud to live off honest folk's labor. They have no shame, couth, or chivalry; they are heartless, loveless, and soon to be (like all of us) pulseless. As for me, I would rather come out of the stands in the new *Roman Colosseum* and join my brothers being fed to the lions and wild dogs!

And so, **I will meet my enemy in the grave like everyone who stands before our mutual Creator.** We will collect the wages for our hands' works and our mouths' words. Because the bones of greater than ours await, they beckon us all!

> *"He that oppresses the poor reproaches his Maker: but he that honors Him has mercy on the poor. The wicked is driven away in his wickedness: but the righteous has hope in his death." **—Solomon, Proverbs 14:31-32***

MANCHURIAN MODEL

IF one thinks a "Manchurian Candidate" is made by force through a brainwashed manipulation of a militant mind, one may have been reading too many books or watched too many movies depicting that sort of *"hard way"* approach to **making spies**. One could get the same results for a few dollars by offering a public position in the lime-light by an off-shore bank account.

Even "fear" or first-time authority can turn close neighbors into spies; the last two years of the COVID biowarfare tactics are proof enough!

There are **many kinds of spies** used for many different applications. Not that one needs to look for "spies" under every rock and behind every tree, but it helps to have a healthy skepticism when facing those in authority who easily subvert the rule of law. Our Canadian Charter of Rights and Freedoms and Constitution is not oppressive; it's the foundation of freedom, but there are those with foreign globalist interests.

(1) Local spies

Sun Tzu taught that the price of sending people to war was so great that it would be "inhumane" to do so without employing spies at any cost. SPIES were understood to be THE ESSENTIAL asset to the *General* and a priceless commodity compared to the price of an empire sending troops at any rate. Thus, the development of spies was more critical than a frontal attack telegraphing one's intent.

And the first spies to be cultivated were "local spies, " winning the locals over by kind privilege and bribes. Heck, jobs after a recession or even **a "Universal Wage" might do the trick!** When people are poor and depressed, even the slightest kindness will be defended and silence any theory or blatant evidence to the contrary.

(2) Inward Spies

Next level, ANY officials, ambitious politicians, greedy high-profile criminals, whom society has punished, those disgruntled, cheated, demoted, and feeling victimized, are the prime candidates as Inward Spies! Holding no allegiance to the nation condemning them, these are hated and rejected by their peers, like the "Hunter Bidens" and the "Justin Trudeaus" of the world. This rolling snowball toward Hell creates further distance from the shore of safety as these ***Inward Spies*** feel vindicated by their ostracization.

(3) Converted Spies

Through the ***recruitment*** by huge bribes and lavish lifestyles, the would-be spies for their own nations get *turned* to do the bidding of the invading forces.

If you want to know who these are, merely follow the money! They have no allegiance to anyone or anything but themselves and their interests! In the past, these *Converted Spies* would have been purchased here and there, but now, because of technological advancement, any multinational corporate CEO has become the greatest spying tool on the planet!

These defend their posture when exposed by blaming underlings and rogue elements in their organizations. They work **hand in hand with rogue 3-Letter Agencies supposed to do their nation's bidding by oath and patriotism.**

(4) Doomed Spies

The invading force must treat all spies and "secret fraternities" with incredible personal respect. Even *secret plans* and complete transparency are rewarded by those entrusted with such a *prestigious mission*. Full disclosure is often mandatory to gain these spies' complete trust, even though they may be caught and tortured for information.

The recruitment department and the spies are fed a narrative of no use in invading the country. At no time is the spy or handler in possession of actual knowledge; they are only provided misleading and leak-detecting information for complete security. If caught or leaks are detected, those spies and receivers of the leaks are terminated.

(5) Surviving Spies

These are people of incredible resilience, superior intellect, physical endurance, and courage; however, on the exterior, they are of low demeanor, grubby, and accustomed to hardships and dirty jobs. These can live as homeless and no-account beggars, as servant class and chauffeur drivers or prostitutes.

Ask politician (USA Democrat) Dianne Feinstein about her nameless Chinese driver and politician Eric Swalwell about his girlfriend "Fang Fang" and determine if they gave up National Secrets? I think that IF just these two examples were privy to State Dept. evidence, it would have long since left the USA with their closest foreign acquaintances. Spies like that probably got a medal for bravery, going beyond their call of duty, especially those like Christine Fang; (Fang).

It could have been the US State Dept. that couldn't trust these two and fed them bogus *intelligence*, maybe because they knew how bought-off and leak-weak they possibly were! Could you imagine a more prime target than our own Prime Minister? You wouldn't have to brainwash that guy; since his youth, he hated Western Canada and deeply respected **China's "basic Dictatorship!"**

My take-away is on the surface; we have this Global Pandemic just after Trump hits China hard, tariffs, and forcing manufacturing back to the USA or pay penalties; thus, sending China's economy into the toilet. Then out of Wuhan comes this Global attack, to be minimized by top Democrats and Fauci himself. They insisted on a complete economic lockdown when that gig was up; if not, millions would die!

Fauci operated without congress or the senate, above POTUS, to be the most powerful man on the planet, and he didn't want to give up his position. But there is more going on; why would *Tony* Fauci, who effectively early-treated the last Coronavirus pandemic with hydroxychloroquine and Vitamin D, leave countless thousands to die by his advice against it? It seems he has more to gain elsewhere.

> "Coronavirus patents speak VOLUMES! Our worst fears may have just recently been proven true. Was coronavirus created as a biological weapon? A lot of us think so"
> **—Unapologetic Republican**
> https://unapologeticrepublican.com/london-real-transform-yourself-blows-lid-off-coronavirus-origin/

> "We know that Anthony Fauci, that Ralph Baric, that the Center for Disease Control and the laundry list of people who wanted

> to take credit for inventing coronavirus were at the hub of this story. From 2003 to 2018, **they controlled 100 percent of the cash flow that built the empire around the industrial complex of coronavirus**."
> —Unapologetic Republican, Coronavirus patents from early 2000 Prove Huge Players Involved In Huge Scheme, **U**Published
> https://rumble.com/vcx0tt-coronavirus-patents-from-early-2000-prove-huge-players-involved-in-huge-sch.html

Amass bio-weapons by WHO political positioning to create a patented virus off-shore in a Wuhan lab with Canadian and US funding;

Bribe the most prominent world producer of therapeutics and vaccines to allow the release of a bio-weapon on an unsuspecting public, forcing them to be locked down on your prison planet, 100% dependent on your information and prescription

Create (as Justin Trudeau said before the entire world) an "opportunity" for the Great Reset! Change the entire Global monetary system with China as the center hub

Detain and force the entire planet by fear to vaccinate and get an ID passport for travel and passage, even though making mandatory Voter ID was proof of racism just *5 minutes* ago!

Electronically grade participants in the New World Order and employ a *"Socialist Credit"* system already enforced in China
Flush any would-be resistance by means of medical assassination, using 'COVID' as the diagnosis for death for any "anti-vaccine" protesters as the world is "overpopulated!"

"**god**-status!" If you think "killing Grandma" by not self-masking outside alone on a beach in 100-degree weather was evil... these corporate sociopaths knock off "Grandma" and then install a death tax (wealth transfer) to go through her pockets before her body even gets cold!

Here is the deal; India reports that much of the China Belt and Road Initiative (BRI) cannot comply with certain obligations. Consequently, many of these countries that have signed "non-binding" contracts under the BRI will still be holding the bag for their investments and promises to China.

These sorts invented the saying, "Promises were meant to be broken!" remember that these Globalist liars only PROMISED the world; those WHO would participate in their diabolical plan—getting the picture yet? It seems that promises made by Gangsters are openly suspect, but promises made by Globalists—not so much?

The planetary death toll mounting over some

preventable virus by early treatment? or untold trillions paid to Pharma companies who are unaccountable; for an ineffective product? Yes, all these seem rantings of a suspicious mind.

Still, even the average skeptic can see the past of the world's "St. Fauci" ridden with animal torture, criminal negligence, medical misconduct, and war crimes! We can guarantee that the worst you think about these corporate psychopaths wouldn't even be the tip of the iceberg! And what does that say about those who would just turn a blind eye?

> "...unholy, without natural affection, trucebreakers, false accusers, incontinent, fierce, despisers of those that are good, Traitors, heady, highminded, lovers of pleasures more than lovers of God; Having a form of godliness..." *2 Timothy 3:3-4*

MANCHURIAN GLOBAL

If appearing weak is a real strategy by Globalist Marxist Superpowers **(making up two-thirds of Earth's nations),** there isn't a more incompetent or weak-looking pawn than Justin Trudeau. **If** his incompetency is merely an act, **if** his blunders are an elaborate deception, **then** this failed drama teacher is starring in his most believable role yet... ***"The Spy Who Groped Me!"***

Like the bumbling numb-scull *"Johnny English"* (unintended insult to "Mr. Bean," the great actor Rowan Atkinson), our Prime Minister' ***JT'*** comes off *cringy and awkward.* Reinventing the trope, in a *clingy,* somewhat *feminine* ditsy *charm* that can ***chameleon*** any color and *ethnicity, pronoun,* or *virtue-signal*—accept for chivalry.

But what I cannot figure out are the pronouns for someone who is *whiter than bread* "identifying" as "Black" or "Brown?" Race dysphoric? Or, Racist, maybe? Which begs the question: What do you get for a guy with multiple personalities? **Oh, that's right, therapy!!** Sadly, as funny as all that may be, it may be too late for Justin to find his identity as a Canadian.

Most Canadians couldn't care less what you identify as or what your associations are; that is, unless, of course, those associations are out to take your property in a "Global Reset" and/or imprison you for **not** wearing a blue M95 sign of submission on your face!

We couldn't care less where you sleep or what you believe unless it is illegal or you force those things on the rest of us! Furthermore, **when they identify as a Globalist after taking an oath as a Prime Minister of CANADA** to defend and uphold our Laws, Charter of Rights, and our National Security or Interests, Trudeau identifies more like a foreign spy or TRAITOR; than anything else!

I would say that Chinese Globalists got their cabinet well picked in the Liberal caucus of "Canada." These **appear** ineffective and incompetent but destroy every fabric of our society and commerce. Creating an economic catastrophe Is one thing, but our Health Care in Canada is being destroyed!

Mandates force out hospital staff, and those who need medical attention are not being treated or are afraid to be treated by a system that has foreign agendas. It would seem that even by a modest appraisal of the forced Vaccine ID program, things aren't going to be "normal" anytime soon!

Far too good of a crisis to let go to waste!

It wouldn't be so bad if Globalist Gangsters showed up and threatened political representatives' *lives* and coerced them by fear of death or blackmail exposure for other crimes they committed. **Instead, they willingly line up to get the first crack at that ticket without any threat.**

> "Justin Trudeau's government...funded coronavirus research project at the Wuhan China virus lab suspected as the source of the deadly plague." —**RebelNews**
> https://www.rebelnews.com/trudeau_research_grant_nearly_one_million_dollars_covid19_research_wuhan_virus_research_laboratory

> "Chinese Donate 1 MILLION to Trudeau Foundation, Trudeau Gets Slammed!!"
> https://www.youtube.com/watch?v=P1J6C3iBzpM

> "Canada supports China's ongoing response to novel coronavirus outbreak" —**Global** Affairs Canada
> https://www.canada.ca/en/global-affairs/news/2020/02/canada-supports-chinas-ongoing-response-to-novel-coronavirus-outbreak.html

> "There is a level of admiration I actually have for China. Because their **basic dictatorship** is allowing them to actually turn their economy around on a dime...."
> —Justin Trudeau

His *heartfelt* sentiment is something that almost 100% of Canadians do not share! I would have given you a video link for that speech, but the nauseating repetitious insertion of his *breathy* ***"ah"*** makes me want to purge every time I am forced to hear it! But it isn't just the Chinese Dictatorship that Trudeau is enamored with, but everyday terrorists like the convicted terrorist murderer Omar Khadr, whom Trudeau secured $10million from our hard-earned tax dollars!

It is one thing to read a headline like *"Trudeau Government Commit OVER 1.5 BILLION DOLLARS To Iraq, Syria"* still, it should have been the last straw when Canadians were forced to swallow *"Trudeau Gave $20 Million In Canadian Taxpayer Money To The Clinton Foundation!"*

The strategy seems to flood the media with so many failures and Canada-destroying policies that they are too innumerable to count. Like The argumentum ad infinitum fallacy, these Liberal policies are like dragging a conversation to *ad nauseam*, only to claim then one's policies and political arguments are correct because no one has been able to contradict them. Like trying to take a glass of water from a FIRE HOSE ...my biggest struggle with writing this book was that I couldn't put the words on the page fast enough to keep up with all the new and tragic Canada-destroying actions our prime minister is taking daily.

Any one of these policies and actions could be demonstrably proven as simply *stupid*, but their total is nothing less than the irreparable devastation of our nation! Put in a bumbling, breathy buffoon to tank our economy, devastate the health of Canadians with counterproductive lockdowns, leaking of our National Security, and the sell-off of our nation's resources by first devaluing them. The Communist Corporate takeover is not just a "conspiracy theory" but an inevitability! By burying us in Chinese debt by incentivizing a welfare state with ***COVID Cash*.**

What about the **"World Commodity Trade Center"** in BC? *WHO* knew that Canada would be China's new North American Hub? Look at the map for the Communist Chinese takeover of Planet Earth and tell me that our Prime Manchurian isn't the ***Reich*** pick for the job! **On the next page** is a picture worth more than a mere thousand words...

http://nacvglobal.com/

[Notice the only two-way arrow]

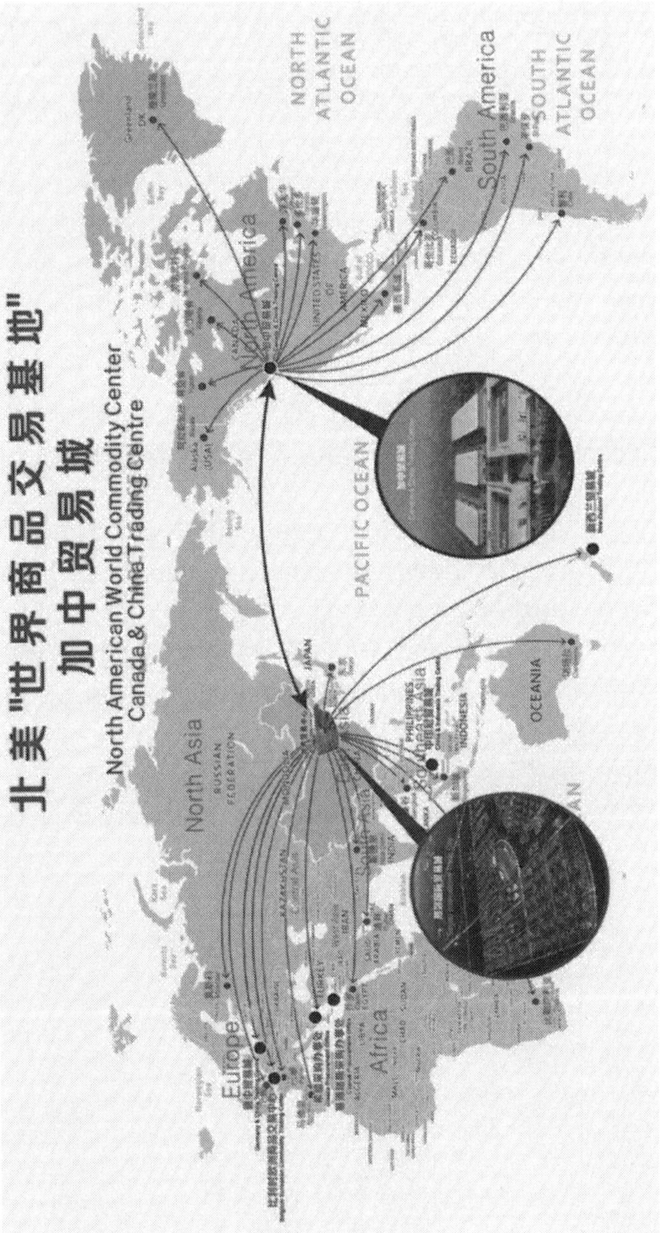
北美"世界商品交易基地"
加中贸易城
North American World Commodity Center
Canada & China Trading Centre
NORTH ATLANTIC OCEAN
SOUTH ATLANTIC OCEAN
PACIFIC OCEAN
North America
South America
North Asia
RUSSIAN FEDERATION
Europe
Africa
OCEANIA
JAPAN
PHILIPPINES
INDONESIA
INDIA
UNITED STATES OF AMERICA

> "**China is paving its *'belt and road'* to British Columbia** - A major warehouse facility under construction in Surrey is not just paving the way for more trade between B.C. and China. It could be helping pave Chinese President Xi Jinping's Belt and Road Initiative to Canada" —Graeme Wood
> https://biv.com/article/2020/08/china-paving-its-belt-and-road-british-columbia

While our Members of Parliament are verbally trouncing the Prime Minister and decrying Liberal lies and the treasonous positions, **JT and gang are laughing all the way to *The Bank of China* at our expense... and probably the cost of our lives!** What place do you think we Canadians will have in that "New World Order?" What do you think?

We who want to keep our national identity and our Rights and Freedoms won't be seen as a threat to **the *Kingdom of Earth's* new Emperor?** How long will it take before the world treats the biblical *Dragon-Serpent* **"Scarlet Beast"** as a *god*?

It's been said that the Marxist infiltration of America is almost complete, with their tentacles reaching as deep and high as politically possible in our Government. You can believe it when top Senators and House Representatives hire and bed Chinese spies with impunity! IF the USA doesn't have a problem with this, it only makes sense that their underbelly is Communist Red! By keeping us focused on the life and times of "the richest men" of the Earth, we have lost sight of WHO may be promoting them!

> "Top Chinese professor boasts of operatives in top of US' core inner circle' ... We have our old friends who are at the top of America's core inner circle of power and influence...for the past 30 years, 40 years, we have been utilizing the core power of the United States" —**Emily Jacobs**
> https://nypost.com/2020/12/08/professor-claims-china-has-people-in-americas-core-inner-circle/

> "**J.R. Nyquist's Introduction**
> What follows is a draft report submitted by a joint committee of the Canadian Security Intelligence Service and the Royal Canadian Mounted Police on the Chinese subversion and penetration of Canada. ...By 1997 Chinese economic involvement in Canada was already too advanced for correction"
> http://www.jrnyquist.com/sidewinder.htm

> "**Manchuria** is an exonym for several large overlapping historical and geographic regions of Russia and China in Northeast Asia (mostly in Northeast China today)."
> https://en.wikipedia.org/wiki/Manchuria

The attacks by this Communist regime amount to the Globe's demise via death by a million paper cuts! Not to be too metaphorical, but each contract signed and handshake amounts to the slow blood-letting of partnerships with **The Beast**. A brain drain, an intelligence drain, a resources drain, and finally, the raising of taxation and interest on those non-forgivable "loans!"

As the not-so proverbial *"Deal with the Devil,"* one can more easily see the demonic entities behind the **Red Dress** of *Liberalism/American Communism*, not to mention a religious (Universal) **Catholicism** that would happily endorse it!

> **"Why Was The Papal Audience Hall Building At The Vatican Constructed In The Shape Of A Giant Reptile?"**
> https://www.nowtheendbegins.com/why-was-the-papal-audience-hall-building-at-the-vatican-constructed-in-the-shape-of-a-giant-reptile/

But that hits a little close; how about we get back to the map we just saw; I want you to notice that there appears to be no trade from China to Russia on the previous map, why you might ask? The "North Asia Russian Federation" is the ***Manchurian*** extension of their mutual Marxist ambitions!

Question: did you know Canada could be liable to compensate Chinese companies for COVID-19 under trade agreements?

"**Canada liable to compensate Chinese companies for COVID-19 losses under Harper govt trade agreement -** "Article 11 of the FIPA states that if Chinese firms in Canada suffer losses due to 'war, state of national emergency, insurrection, riot or other similar events,' they can sue the Canadian Government for compensations," https://thinkpol.ca/2020/04/20/canada-liable-compensate-chinese-companies-covid-19-losses-harper-govt-trade-agreement/

"***Canada has become a battleground on which the Chinese Communist Party seeks to terrorize, humiliate and neuter its opponents***" ***-Aurthur Johnathan Manthorpe***" —Terry Glavin, https://nationalpost.com/opinion/terry-glavin-its-official-china-is-a-threat-to-canadas-national-security

"Trojan horse" strategy to gain influence in "many parts of the world." "**They penetrate the economies**, they buy up everything they can, pay off everybody they can... then make demands..."—**Abigail Ng, Jan 13,** 2020–https://www.cnbc.com/2020/01/13/china-is-the-most-serious-threat-to-the-united-states-james-jones.html

MANCHURIAN DREAM

Disney paints China as a hotpot-serving, panda-loving nation of math wizards that are all good at martial arts, strong in precise military might, and are intellectually superior technological giants. Furthermore, we were taught in school that Canada has a long-standing relationship with China; after all, "they already built our railroads!" What a racist insult to the Chinese people as if their practically forced labor identifies them. But suppose we should dare get a conscience; in that case, our boring, peace-loving *Canadian* media will cancel or crush anyone skeptical of a China Belt and Road Initiative (BRI) that can only *"benefit"* Canadians.

> "By the time the railway was completed in 1885, **fervent anti-Chinese racism in British Columbia** impelled the introduction of the federal Chinese Head Tax that year. ...Chinese exclusion halted population growth to approximately 32,000 by the time the Act was repealed in 1947."
> https://www.thecanadianencyclopedia.ca/en/article/segregation-of-asian-canadians

I want to clarify that any reference to Communist China is my opinion on its political aspirations at the cost of many Chinese lives and others who may oppose its Marxism. I would also point out that historically the Canadian Government had more in common with some of the oppressive dictatorships of the world, but also something not taught in schools.

We have heard of the Residential Schools, but how many have heard of the British Columbian Doukhobor children similarly taken? Taking children from their parents seems to be the Canadian Government and RCMP way! They did this upon refusal to send their children to school; **what if you refuse their Global Vaccine?**

Don't worry; they will "apologize" later and toss some devalued cash to the survivors in a few years. Easier to get *forgiveness* than permission.
IF school were a place for balanced learning and not a cesspool of indoctrination, it would be a perfect place for children to get a practical education on living in reality. We could learn of the historical roots of countries (like our own) and appreciate its foundational lessons like getting a trade, balancing a checkbook, proper non-GMO nutrition, and complete family appreciation.

I sincerely appreciate the Chinese people and their heritage because their language seems to reveal the foundation of my biblical faith. Considering China, I believe that nation has some of the richest histories, having the oldest language that ultimately upheld biblical tradition from its inception. That's right; ancient Chinese is biblical!

The following are a few examples of how the ancient Chinese language holds the key to the Genesis of the Bible; our genesis and beginning:

> "Chinese Characters and Genesis on March 6, 1998, Here are seven Chinese Characters that show that the ancient Chinese knew the Gospel message found in the book of Genesis. In the book God's Promise to the Chinese by Ethel R. Nelson and Richard E. Broadberry, hundreds more are revealed..." —Answers In Genesis
> https://answersingenesis.org/genesis/chinese-characters-and-genesis/

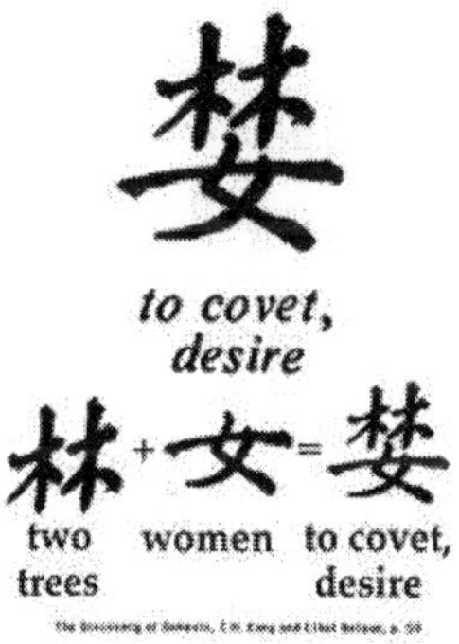

The word for "covet" or the temptation of desire reveals the picture of two trees in the Garden of

Eden, where a woman (Eve) succumbed to her desire for the tree of knowledge of good and evil. And what is significant about the word for "boat" is that it depicts the story of Noah and the Ark, where only eight people were saved from the global flood.

The following word for "to create" shows a combination of words that picture speaking life into dust, and life walking and mud... as man was created from the dust and made a living soul from that mud by the word spoken by God! The ancient Chinese language is based on the same oral traditions that we find compiled in the Biblical record. Amazingly, the oldest culture on Earth mirrors the Genesis account, and the word for "complete" pictures that first couple in Eden.

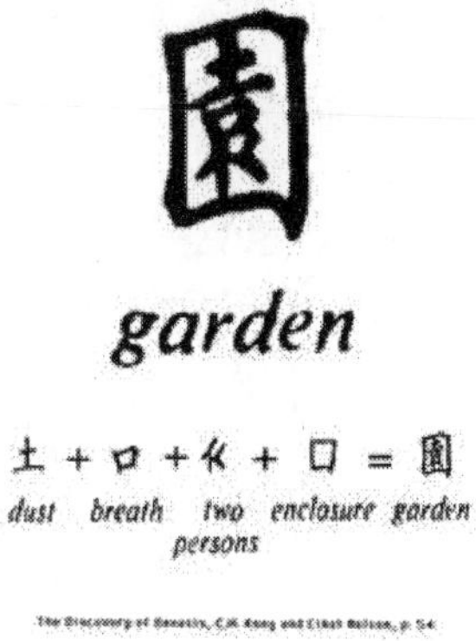

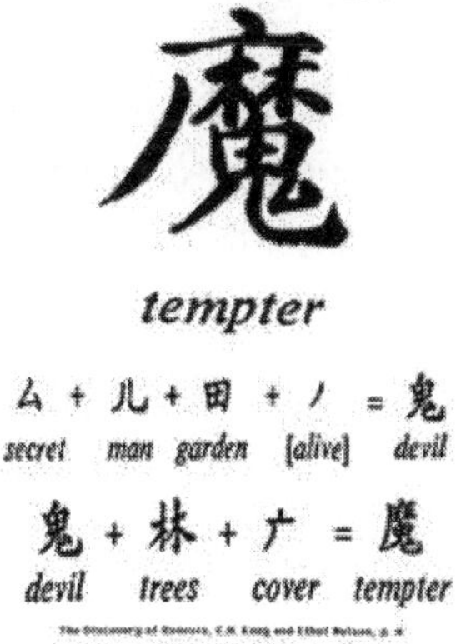

Kang, C.H., The Discovery of Genesis Concordia Publishing House. Kindle Edition. *"The Discovery of Genesis: How the Truths of Genesis Were Found Hidden in the Chinese Language Paperback – August 1, 1979 by C. H. Kang (Author), Ethel R. Nelson In this linguistic analysis, the two distinguished authors dissect Chinese characters to reveal that, according to their research, the ancient Chinese were aware of the God of Abraham and the Chinese were,*

> *possibly, a remnant of the Tower of Babel dispersion. The authors break down Chinese characters to provide a visual for learning how the story of the world's creation by the One True God is evident in the Chinese language." Kang, C.H.. The Discovery of Genesis . Concordia Publishing House. Kindle*
> https://www.amazon.com/Discovery-Genesis-Truths-Chinese-Language/dp/0570037921

Maybe I'm seeing what I want to see as a *Western* Christian, but the word for God looks much like a few pictures in one. A ***spike***, a ***cross***, and *a* ***plaque*** of declaration—like the one that Pontius Pilate put over the head of Christ as crucified on the cross! What a rich picture of the revelation of Christ in God! What hope for humanity, a reminder that we will all stand before our Creator to give an account of our lives here in His world.

神

SHEN, GOD

My question is simple; why haven't we been taught THIS in school? Why hasn't National Geographic featured THIS as a cover story? **Why hasn't CBC done a full-on documentary on THIS biblical connection?** Where is the Disney Movie? Maybe they don't know about it, or they would instead float some other narrative that would go along with a political party that would erase God if it could. It makes you wonder why? Doesn't it?

Why have Marxist/Communist regimes constantly attacked believers in God? What is so intimidating about God that they must take extreme measures to crush those who believe in Him? Why spend so much effort trying to stop or overthrow Him if God doesn't exist? It has been said that...

"Without God, atheists wouldn't exist!"

I don't expect our media to cover these topics more than Buddhism, Maoism, Taoism, and Hinduism, **but no love for Jesus?** Even "Christmas" is getting the boot from the mainstream media! Also, this is a sensitive subject for some people because who knows what would happen if more people were aware of the atrocities committed behind The Great Wall? WHO knows what kind of PR nightmare it would be if the world didn't want that kind of future for their children? They may start buying local, one toy, one truck, or tanker at a time! It isn't the persecution of religious belief in

God, but which god! Globalists want world domination by replacing God with themselves!

When China makes it lucrative for the Media to ***retreat to safety*** without battling for the people oppressed under Communism, why would anyone want to forge ahead into a costly war of words? But the crazy thing is, people need to ask themselves how they will be treated under that regime when they steamroll over us? No one will be there to fight for our worthless lives! The "alarm bells" were sounded 30 years ago, but they have gone unheeded or silenced! IF the blood of millions under those kinds of brutal, oppressive dictatorships has been a lesson for us to learn, why does the press continually ignore it?

For the life of them, mice just cannot figure out why the cheese is free!

It doesn't enter their entitled little minds; somehow, their entitlement mentality drives their appetites and addictions to a predictable demise. No matter how many smashed heads of previous mice, strewn bodies torn apart by the traps of "prosperity," it goes unnoticed!

The mindless greed of getting without earning, the desire to steal from those who worked for each dime by smarts or sweat; raped and pillaged so we can enjoy our "universal income?" ...is to be deserving of the bloody traps that await! If one thinks that the rich deserve these goods by theft, what voice do you think the poor will have when even the rich and powerful get silenced?

This whole "Belt and Road Initiative" seems like an incredible **"golden bridge to retreat across,"** ...leaving our Sovereignty and National Security behind by amassing unsustainable debt in trade for our resources and our very citizenship! **Why aren't our "Representatives" warning us?** Surely, they are privy to classified material that would make this book seem like "Sesame Street!" So why don't Journalists blow the whistle on what our Government is doing? **Because they aren't whistleblowers... they are WHISTLE SUCKERS!**

> *"If we lose freedom here,* ***there is no place to escape to.*** *This is the last stand on earth." – Ronald Reagan*

It is too easy to sleep at night, as we don't give those in prisons in cold rat-infested quarters a second thought. **But sleep flees from them as they wake all night in prayer for us, that we don't end up in the same fate they are forced to endure!** The same promises of "great" Socialism and Communism were promised to them, now, their organs are harvested, and their children work in squalor to make us more stuff. I have always said communes are *a great idea*, as long as you are the one in control!

What kind of blind arrogance must we have not to use our freedom to cry for those who cannot be heard? But instead, use our incredible wealth **to reward those** who torture others ... who will be us; it's just a matter of time!

Keep in mind it's not that temptations are so great; it is just that our will and the fabric of our character is so weak.

> "...you shall take no *gift*: for the gift blinds the wise, and perverts the words of the righteous." —Moses, Exodus 23:8

I have always had a deep respect and interest in indigenous peoples and their historical cultures. It speaks to me of the resilience and adaptability to survive and thrive under sad oppression. China holds some of humanity's most diverse and foundational historical records, reaching back as far as written history can go, establishing oral tradition and many of the earliest ancient religions we appreciate today.

Language and culture aim to educate and ingrain principles into our generations. Unfortunately, today's greed seems to forget oaths and traditions that preserved our nation for such a day; a pledge without trust is fraud.

Such greed seems to give little acknowledgment to those who paid in blood, sweat, and even a river of tears by those who merely wanted to live peaceful lives and preserve such for their children. The Chinese gave their children to work and wars to keep what they had in hopes of a better tomorrow. These were honorable souls among many diverse cultural families representing their village, province, and nation! Such a testimony of earlier days is the *Naxi* culture.

In the name “Naxi,” we find how prophetic *names* have endured the tests of time and trial; Na means ‘older and honorable’ and Xi means people. One cannot find a better word to testify such enduring roots to face the storms.

Are China's leaders Chinese? Does the current leadership of China represent its heritage? Why does this nation pay tribute to a German character (Marx) who controls their modern politics? Will the souls of those who have died for thousands of years, knowing what awaits, approve the aspirations of this post-cultural China?

In 2018 on the 200th anniversary of the birth of Carl Marx, a German philosopher, Xi Jinping, gave a speech at the Great Hall of the People in Beijing to celebrate his apparent political mentor and idol in Marx. I watched the entire address to the young leadership of China, and I must say it was a sad discovery. The video cameras only took snippets of Xi Jinping but spent most of the time panning the attendees in **a close-up investigation of each face**, every movement, and reaction to every statement.

From commencement to completion, not a smile, not a nod of agreement or look of inspiration; only serious robotic looks and some taking notes until it ended. **What a sad and sorry spectacle.**

When it did end (over an hour later), the thousands in the crowd erupted into euphoric applause; now, there wasn't a face without a smile or gleeful expression! Curious. Was it the final relief of a torturous hour plus forced indoctrination session? Was it the programmed response to a programmed speech for a programmed audience? Was it a mass formation psychosis? Possibly, forced insanity of those given wholly to the teachings of a 200-year-old German philosophy, now summing up the culmination of China's existence, achievements, and future?

No other philosophy, no historical marker for future progression; no religion and hint of personal expression; only cold materialism and the worship of human achievement in that cult of Carl Marx. What a sad betrayal.

Is this why China bled to survive?

While Xi Jinping makes a national celebration to honor the birth of Carl Marx, I find it curious that this now great leader of China couldn't find someone as rich a model among his own people? **Not even one** to commemorate and celebrate as a founder or great heroic model for today's China? Is this the dream of China? **Or its nightmare?** In summary, is China now to be represented by a German foreigner? A mere two-hundred-year-old German philosophy?
From Naxi to Nazi? **What a shame.**

See what awaits the world under a New World Order? One's every move must get monitored and every expression cataloged for signs of independence. Where **their prescription is compliance, and their mandate is obedience!** Each word must be memorized and studied during every speech by Globalist Dictators, and every FREE and Radical brain cell destroyed!

The look of depression and forced compliance was undeniable; the only thing that wasn't visible was the gun to their heads causing such performance!

Joe Rogan: "I just don't understand how it gets to the point where..." **Jordan Peterson:** "Things get to terrible places one tiny step at a time. If I encroach on you, and I'm sophisticated about it, I am going to encroach 2 millimeters. I'm going to encroach right to the point where you start to protest. Then I'm going to stop. Then I'm going to wait. Then you're going to calm down, and I'm going to encroach again right to the point where you protest. Then I'm going to stop; then I'm going to wait. Then I'm just going to do this forever, and before you know it, you're going to be back three miles from where you started, and I'll have done this one step at a time. Then you'll go, 'Oh, how did I get here?' And the answer was, well, I pushed you a little further than you should've gone. And you agreed. And so then I pushed you a little farther than you should have gone again, and you agreed. And if anybody is interested in this sort of process, and this is a horrifying book, if you want to read about how this process works, you can read a book called "Ordinary Men" by Robert Browning."—Joe Rogan, with Jordan Peterson | The Post Millennial https://rumble.com/vqf7yb-things-get-to-better-places-one-tiny-step-at-a-time.html

THE MANCHURIAN CANADIAN

IT would take volumes of books to address the undermining of our Democracy by teachers we have entrusted with our education. The legal systems we have tasked with our disagreements, the media with our information, and politicians we have charged with our governance. But it all boils down to the arbitrary deviations outside the definition of what it means to be Canadian.

Does the modern Canadian view themselves as a Canadian Citizen, or has the indoctrination done its work? And now we answer to a "higher authority" as a "global citizen?" And no longer one who, by birth or by choice, has a collective obligation to further the prospects and security of their Nation.

A "Postnational" society is another name for Globalism! Where you not only lose your national identity, you lose all property, rights, and freedoms, protected by those same national constitutions and charters! This war for our freedoms is fought and won by our conquest or consent without firing a shot! The State vanquishes your vote, your voice, and your volition.

The means of this is accomplished by a promise; I repeat, only the **promise** of a Socialist welfare system. IT PROMISES "free stuff" by global welfare to anyone who would give up their national rights and God-given freedoms. What would typically take all-out war to accomplish in past years is now **by Marxist *indoctrinated* citizens, demanded.**

WHO is behind all this, the UN is behind all this, and the 6 Globalist Communist Controllers of all media are behind all this! Because National Identity is the only thing standing between us and their agenda for us.

> "Postnationalism or non-nationalism is the process or trend by which nation states and national identities lose their importance relative to cross-nation and self-organized or supranational and global entities as well as local entities."
> **—Wikipedia, the free encyclopedia,**
> https://en.wikipedia.org/wiki/Postnationalism

> "The highest form of warfare is one, in which the enemy is conquered, without shots being fired. War by attrition, infiltrating the adverserial nation, then weaken and demoralize it by engineering conflicts within it can lead to its self destruction... The communist dictatorships that adapted the Marxist ideology in the 20th Century – Soviet Union, China, Vietnam, the former Eastern Bloc, Cuba, North Korea – became the most repressive

regimes. An estimated 100 Million died, as a result of executions, famine, or labor camps and 1 Billion were enslaved – and many still are – in those totalitarian states."
—The Enemy Within: Part 1. Marxist Infiltration of America
https://timefortruth.blog/2020/09/28/the-enemy-within-part-1-marxist-infiltration-of-america

"Cultural Marxism is disguised in the United States, as liberalism, or progressivism. Liberty and progress are positive concepts, so this must be good for us, right? Let's see what's behind some of this "progress"."—The Enemy Within: Part 2 Marxist Subversion of America,
https://timefortruth.blog/2020/10/06/the-enemy-within-part-2-marxist-subversion-of-america/

"The goal of Cultural Marxism, that infiltrated America during the 20th Century, is to overthrow the Western democracy from within, without firing a shot. Using stealth and deception instead of force, the strategy is to transform the consciousness of society by taking control of the flow of information, the media, education, entertainment and publishing."
—The Enemy Within: Part 3. Marxist Division of America
https://timefortruth.blog/2020/10/15/the-enemy-within-part-3-marxist-division-of-america/

It seems we are ***"ahead"*** of our American neighbors here in Canada, now recognized as a "Socialist" country. More taxes and less traditional, cultural, and religious freedoms; are forced on our multicultural citizenry. Cultural Marxism has thoroughly permeated the CBC (our State-owned Media) and 4/5 of our political choices. There are five leading political parties in Canada: The Conservative Party, The Liberal Party, The Green Party, The New Democratic Party (NDP), and Le Bloc Quebecois. The Conservative Party and the People's Party of Canada (PPC) are the only parties that favor smaller governments and the delegation of more provincial power. The Conservatives and the PPC were the only non-globalist options among the top parties until **Erin O'Toole** sabotaged the conservatives but, thankfully, was booted!

One would have thought that at least Le Bloc Quebecois would have positioned themselves as independent of Global Reset Lockdowns, but, they have revealed themselves as the most fascist defenders of Globalism State-Sponsored tyranny.

Tearing a page out of the Globalist playbook is creating a crisis and providing the cure. First, mandate the mayhem and then mobilize the troops to enforce Martial Law! Even the Conservative Party is getting weak in the knees when it comes to representing the will of Canadians will; because the growing populations are showing signs of acquiescence to a Globalist Marxist welfare Statehood. **Is it too late?** At least Le Bloc voted against the Emergencies (War) Measures Act with Conservatives.

> "A nation can survive its fools and even the ambitious, but it cannot survive treason from within... for the traitor moves among those within the gates freely"..." He rots the soul of a nation, he works secretly and unknown in the night to undermine the pillars of a city." — Cicero

IF you thought this book was about bashing Trudeau, you would be wrong! It is about exposing the infection that merely has gone viral throughout his *ruling-class kind* and is now making its way throughout the ignorant middle and lower working classes. Like the plandemic, climate change, global economic failure, and more, any of which would eat our lunch on any given day.

1) create the crisis, manufacture the mayhem
2) present the problem, all Media in unison censoring any word or dissenting thought
3) supply the ONLY solution, the *"Global Savior,"* without question or comment! Then offer the "Golden Gate" through which we can retreat or face social cancellation, fines, or imprisonment...
but on the other side, COMMUNIST UTOPIA...

THE PROMISE of PROSPERITY!

How is this possible? Every Canadian politician is in a position of authority, seeing themselves in their political identity instead of their citizenship! We don't need "spies" to infiltrate our country and divulge our most cherished matters of National Security; we already have our military and government planning "cold weather warfare" **with China**, the most significant global threat!

For the most part, **the *Canadian* police officer sees themselves as an arm of the current political party** instead of defenders of their sworn duty to uphold Laws and Statutes established by our Constitution and Charter of Rights to "serve and protect" Canada and her peoples! Many Canadian voters see themselves as Global citizen, only to discover they have become useful idiots and sell-outs that will end in their own demise as enslaved, voiceless, nameless penniless drones!

My point is if *Canadians* think they have no voice now out of 38 Million and growing, wait till they are only one voice in 8 Billion! And when they take away the painstaking effort of even going to a ballot box at those numbers, especially during the **plandemic season!** THEY have already given us a phone by which THEY know our affiliation and will establish that only THEY *can be trusted* with the world's future. In **hindsight**, that model worked quite well for the Marxist Globalists in the last **2020 American election**.

MARX OF THE BEAST

Only people ignorant of history cannot see that Marxism is our enemy. It is an enemy whose clear intent cannot be seen by those destined to repeat history, but when you see it, you are too late! The enemy is not stupid or lazy; they are willing to work late and rise early; they are eager to invest in their future and protest in the street! And their foe? Their foe is weak; otherwise, they wouldn't be their foe! Marxists only attack the weak and lazy, much like the hyena or coyote who will attack the sick, isolated and diseased.

The Marxists cannot win against one who is rational, moral, and studied; they must rely on the psychosis, selfish ambition, and their patrons' utter ignorance of history.

They say that the more "intellectual" and "wealthy" you are, the easier it is for you to accept the Marxist mindset. Not to simplify the complexity of such "deep or woke" individuals, but it all contributes to the "greater good" of the close-minded focus of Marxism. In that world, you are not as intellectual as you might project because your thoughts and actions must eventually submit to the "greater good," which someone else will determine. A sort of superiority and elitism becomes the self-deluded; the very position they think they hold in society is the same class that is to be erased!

I have a (work-wealthy) friend who claims to love communism because he wants everyone locked down for fear of COVID until you explain the results of Communism. Then he comes back with some exclamation, "I am not *really* a 'Communist'; I am more of a Socialist!" and BTW, "Canada is a Socialist country!" That rationale can only shuffle the deluded faster toward their destined Gulag!

I have a question for those who oppose the free speech of their political adversaries: who will be there to defend your right to free speech when it too becomes irrelevant, intolerable, and illegal? This enemy's clear intent will not be seen by those destined to repeat history, but when they do see it, it will be too late!

Quibbling about the concepts, differences, and theoretical Communism and Socialism never addresses the application of both. It is an ideology, never applied the way it is supposed to work; making people "equal" ... always seems to make some more "equal" than others!

Even if it were to make everyone "equal," there could be no reward for excellence and no natural consequence for dereliction of duty. Like examples of *Christianity*, either you have the biblical version of Christianity or the hypocritical perversion of it! Either it applies the teachings of Christ, or it doesn't. Most people only understand a surface concept of Communism/Socialism ***as it is sold*** and do not know the actual foundational tenants.

"10 Planks of The Communist Manifesto"
www.beliefnet.com/columnists/watchwomanonthewall/2011/07/list-of-10-planks-of-the-communist-manifesto.html

- Abolish private property.
- Levy high progressive income tax.
- Abolish inheritance.
- Confiscate property of emigrants & rebels.
- Centralize & monopolize credit & banks.
- Control communication, transportation & media.
- Remove private ownership of factories/business
- Equalize labor.
- Monopolize & subsidize agriculture & industry.
- Control education by socialist indoctrination.

> "**10 Planks of Communism** - Karl Marx describes in his Communist Manifesto, the ten steps necessary to destroy a free enterprise system and replace it with a system of unlimited government power, so as to effect a communist socialist state."
> https://www.jeremiahproject.com/culture-war/10-planks-communism/
>
> (more on this later)

"Hitler Was a Socialist Who Learned from **Karl Marx**. Here Are the Quotes to Prove It" —Chris Talgo| 6, 2020
https://stoppingsocialism.com/2020/07/hitler-was-a-socialist-who-learned-from-karl-marx/

"Pierre Trudeau was a Communist - Trudeau apparently was inspired in Moscow. He couldn't wait to get home, where he began writing pro-Soviet articles. ...Before dawn on October 16, 1970, Communist Pierre Trudeau invoked the War Measures Act, suspended the Canadian Bill of Rights, and imposed a dictatorship on Canada. Trudeau now had the power of censorship, for instance, and could search without warrant and arrest without trial." Monday, 24 December 2018
https://historylessonsdeleted.blogspot.com/2018/12/pierre-trudeau-was-communist.html

Some would contest that Christianity is like Communism or Socialism. Yet any reference in (Luke 4.18) for the release of captives, freeing the oppressed, the forgiveness of debt, or sharing wealth is by the Spirit of God, inspiring one's own (not government-regulated) *charity*.

The entire premise of *generosity* is unnecessary in a "Communist/Socialist State" because everyone is supposed to be "equal" and receive fair treatment.

So, one should not have more needs than the other, and one should not have more possessions, **but that is never practiced**. Compare Communist China or Russian envoys; they are dispatched with far more pomp and prestige ...than their peasant citizen serfs!

> "You Can Be A Christian, You Can Be A Marxist, But You Can't Be Both - to spout neo-Marxist talking points while claiming to walk with Jesus Christ does a gross disservice to the Good News of the Gospel."—Joshua Lawson
> https://thefederalist.com/2020/06/11/you-can-be-christian-you-can-be-marxist-but-you-cant-be-both/

Half of the world is presently occupied by Socialist Nations, either by consent or conquest. These nations bear the burden of an ideology that seeks not the freedom of humanity but its dominance. Under socialism, people are *free* to obey the State, *consent to whatever the State dictates, and* say whatever is sanctioned by the State.

That is not freedom! Somehow the West is brainwashed into thinking that theoretical Socialism is a Utopia, but all evidence to the contrary proves power corrupts, and absolute power corrupts absolutely! Somehow the dreamy philosophy is always preserved by traitors of all that is humane. Such as these, go through the pockets of the ***dead***, and point the gun against the ***head*** of anyone not sufficiently ***red***.

> "Power tends to corrupt, and absolute power corrupts absolutely. Great men are almost always bad men." —Lord Acton, Letter to Bishop Mandell Creighton in 1887

These are the sorts who think that freedom is a curse and that the problems that arise from choice are too great a burden for commoners to carry.

I have been with my family on road trips with my old *resurrected* "65 Schoolie" and "68 Fishbowl" ...from Canada to Guatemala, through some of the poorest communities to help build homes. I can say that the generosity and love you get from some who can barely afford a smile is the closest thing to genuine humanity that you will ever experience. But don't get it twisted; their blessed example is not because of their oppression but due to their soul *being exposed* through malnutritioned bodies.

My arms have carried a weak, sick man weighing no more than 80lbs down a riverbank and across a rocky shore just so that he could witness a family Church baptism, using his last loving energy to support their faith.

It is a day when faith in God and the faith in your fellow oppressed is all you have left. A day when your government ***"representatives"*** live lavishly on your labor and poverty; it's a stark reminder of how resilient the human soul is **and how wretched the human condition can get because of greed.**

"Religion is the opium of the people," Karl Marx said, and I wonder why? After he was looking on in agreement to breaking their bones and confiscating their property, **even Marx could see the healing effects and soothing attributes of faith!** Are we to encourage such barbarian Marxism that squeezes the life, blood, and faith out of such beautiful souls? Because that is the future of Canadian Socialism!

> "Faith is the substance of things hoped for, the evidence of things not seen."
>
> Hebrews 11:1

Just because you ***vote in a dictator (like Trudeau in Canada)*** **doesn't mean you live in a free nation!** When governments can fabricate or manufacture a crisis just to override the freedoms of Citizens that don't affect the traitorous Politicians who did so, you can't call that democratic! It's been said, *"You Can Vote Your Way Into Socialism, But You Have To Shoot Your Way Out"* **...question: out to where?**

"Marxism is dead everywhere
—except American universities!"

That was the running joke after the Soviet Union fell in 1991, but only after 100 million people were slaughtered under communism. 31 years later, communism has spread from the universities into mainstream education, media, and Deep State politics. What was once radical has now been embraced as woke ideals for a New World Order.

> "Why... between 1992 and 2006, did China and the USA used to be able to settle all kinds of issues? No matter what kind of crisis we encountered, be it the Yinhe incident, the bombing of the embassy, or the crashing of the plane, things were resolved in no time like (a couple) do with their quarrels starting at the bedhead but ending at the bed end. We fixed everything in two months. What is the reason?
>
> I am going to throw out something maybe a little bit explosive here. It is just because we have people at the top. At the top of America's core inner circle of power and influence, we have our old friends. For the past 30 years, 40 years, we have been utilizing the core power of the United States." –Di Dongsheng, Bejing Professor
> https://www.youtube.com/watch?v=3xa-w2MTKRA

America will be dead everywhere
–precept of Marxist universities!

DON'T CALL THEM LIBERALS

All the lobbying (taking bribes) from Globalist Communists, bankrupting our nation, and training our adversaries' armies on our native land; **YES,** the government has become our enemy!

As far back as I can remember, my father voted Liberal. At least it seemed that way by how he defended the party. We used to have some lively go-arounds! I would rant about some conservative, and he would tell me how crooked he was! And I would tell him how dishonest his guy was; then my father would say how the conservatives were out to starve the country. And away we would go to that tune or another. But, we both had a commonality: we couldn't stand the NDP!

Those guys seemed to leave scorched earth of fiscal destruction in their wake, and it would take years to recover from that *kind of socialism.* If you were to tell the former generation the kind of Marxist Globalism these "Liberals" have in store for Canada... they would burn their registration!!

Our countryman didn't die serving our nation just to have a globalist puppet bankrupt our country and hand us over to be governed by a foreign nation or nations! What has happened to the Canada we were raised to honor and defend? What about the oaths these "public servants" pledged? Did we somehow miss the memo? We cannot even re-call these traitors! "Glorious and free?" *Does W.H.O. stand* on guard for thee? Where is the "True patriot love?"

What is some proof that Canadians are about to be taken over by China or a Castro-communist event? Is there some evidence of Justin's treason?

> "Trudeau govt funds China biolab linked to origin of pandemic almost $1M for coronavirus research ...The grant, linked to the University of Alberta, will help 'team members' at the Wuhan Institute of Virology to perform tests"
> https://www.lifesitenews.com/news/trudeau-govt-funds-china-biolab-linked-to-origin-of-pandemic-almost-1m-for-coronavirus-research/

> "Trudeau is giving China access to Canadian national secrets and giving them a military advantage over democratic nations..."
> —SPENCER FERNANDO
> https://spencerfernando.com/2017/03/28/treason-trudeau-just-sold-canadas-national-security-china/

There isn't enough paper to list the possible bribes, family ties, and political favors; Trudeau has engaged as the only PM who has broken ethics laws. His tenure is a **stain** on Canada's history and future. What seems evident to the world now calling Canada a "Socialist country" is lost on the everyday Canadian trying to make a living. But as practical Communism goes, it seems we have all the earmarks now of a dictatorship, using the COVID lockdowns to hold travelers in internment camps. Canadian internment camps! **What the?**

We now have no freedom of association or movement in our own "free" country! Who will help us? The USA? Huh! Joe Biden is on the Chinese payroll too!

It was hard to tell if Justin Trudeau was a front for Islamic Terror or if he was merely inept. Don't let his *simple* demeanor fool you; he is a brutal, bloody hatchling dictator because we finally know he will only do what is expedient to his globalist handlers. First COVID lockdowns to vaccines, then maybe food shortage to Bill Gates formula! Yeah, what about Bill Gates? It seemed like yesterday he was building viruses to infect computers, then selling the anti-virus. I wonder what he is up to now?

Back to our fair-haired *child-soldier*; you know they make the most brutal, heartless kind. Look at Fidel Castro when he was young! That guy could shoot you as to look at you. It seems Trudeau would have us before some *vaxxation* firing squad!

As long as we see Justin Trudeau (JT) as a fool, we will overlook the genius behind the globalists' choice. Canada has less than 40 million people and is politically inert. Easy enough to overthrow the nation in broad daylight with such a combination. How? When our Parliament can crow all day long about the illegal and dangerous practices of our Liberal government, only to be met with diversion and comedic rebuttal with no change or accountability whatsoever, we are TOAST! Have you ever watched that charade? **Pierre Poilievre wipes the floor with the Liberal body of lies, but the only thing we get is a chuckle?!**

Before Pierre Poilievre, there was Rona Ambrose; either one of those two would have made excellent patriotic leaders of our nation. But instead, we get Beavis and Butt-Head, and you can take your pick of the Liberal cabinet to fill those slots.! It seems to matter little how those seats fill.

The result is the same; we are headed for a Globalist Reset to disenfranchise each Canadian vote for a global consensus instead. We need strong Canadians and more police and military to honor their pledge to serve and protect our flag and Nation! But sadly, we have the World Health Organization (WHO) as dictator.

Our citizenship is Canadian. Are we willing to be true to that birthright or vowed allegiance? If not, why don't we find another place to live, do business, and riot? Canada has been a peace-loving nation that some may call boring, but Canadians have enjoyed all kinds of governance without blatant tyranny **until now**. We have enjoyed the smartest and the stupidest political representatives, and we have survived. Yet what seems to be coming down the pipe is a bomb!

The "journalists" are trying to be measured as not to alienate their subscribers. The "news" outlets are talking about some random "Royalty Scandal" (but not the one with the pedophiles), and at all costs, avoid talking about the Chinese hostile takeover of Canada!

Suppose average everyday citizens of our nation can see the money laundering, bribery, and political favors transferred in broad daylight. How is it that the news cannot report on it in Canada? Other nations' media report on our *Communist* Government aspirations as threats to their National Security!? Because specific policies this "Liberal Party" has instituted have left the world to consider if resistance to Communist China is a futility worth the effort.

Meanwhile, we rant about our political parties as though we had time on our side. We don't. While we are eating popcorn and watching the show, **the theater is on fire**, and the law-abiding types that we are, no one is alarming the ticket holders of their demise!

> "We need to stop calling them liberals and begin referring to them as exactly what they are: American communists, that wish to partake in the destruction of western civilization." —**Candace Owens**
>
> *New York Times* Bestseller "Blackout: How Black America Can Make Its Second Escape from the Democrat Plantation" —**Candace Owens**

I remember the first time I saw Candace Owens on her YouTube channel *"Red Pill Black,"* wondering if this was real? This woman is amazing! Shattering all the myths peddled by the Media being swallowed by the public. I told my wife in the next room, "You gotta see this!" What a blast! She was tired of the lies and deception forced on Blacks every election cycle and exposed self-loathing White Liberals as the racists they are... expecting less of Black America! **Boom!**

I believe our North America is finally waking up to the Kool-Aid we have been forced to drink; in our schools, workplaces, and homes! So refreshing to hear people taking *"the Media to Church!"*

We have many great black conservatives and media sensations defending true American liberty:

HUD Secretary Dr. Ben Carson, Justice Clearance Thomas, Lt. Col Allen West, David Webb, and Larry Elder, Candice Owens, Thomas Sowell, Walter Williams, James T. Harris, David Harris Jr., and Leo Terrell to name a few. These men and women aren't "re-shaping" America; they are reviving America to uphold its foundational morals and ideals! These truths are self-evident and a promise for everyone in their nation to pray for and expect nothing less, from those who hold down a job to those who hold public office who call themselves American! Canadians could use a bit more of THAT.

Communism is **not** your friend. You can dress it up, but you can't take it anywhere you want to keep your freedom. ***Catastrophe*** is out of the bag **...a *Liberal* by any other name is still a Communist!**

We still don't get it; every exposed ***failure*** that Conservatives log against Liberals is a proud ***win*** on their part. We see it as their treasonous crimes destroying our nation; they see it as a good start! As Candace Owens said, they **"wish to partake in the destruction of western civilization."** And the worst thing is that it drips down to a local level where some neighbors are empowered to enforce that tyranny. Somehow they feel more secure enforcing lockdowns, mandates, and compliance; like a proverbial *teacher's pet*, they long for power and approval. And that local Bylaw Officer *shining up his boots* on your simple life, now it's their time!

Socialism: You have two cows.
The government takes one and gives it to your neighbor.

Communism: You have two cows.
The government takes both of them and forces you to milk them for some milk.

Fascism: You have two cows.
The government takes both of them, then sells you some milk.

Nazism: You have two cows.
The government takes both of them and then shoots you.

Marxism: You do not have any cows.
The World Economic Forum—"You'll own nothing. And you'll be "*happy*."

Capitalism: You have two cows.
You sell one and buy a bull. Do the work, get lots of milk, beef, and happiness!

Truism: Don't act like a cow, don't take anyone's bull, and drink lots of milk. Why milk? Because it's good for your teeth. Know what else is good for your teeth? Minding your own business!

WESTERN COMMUNISTS

Marxism capitalizes on the greed of the weak against the integrity of the strong. It rewards mindless, heartless compliance, destroying curiosity and free thought by lavishly bribing spies against their fellow citizens. These are weak-willed and cannot empathize with those caring for children and the working class just trying to live under an oppressive government!

Communists treat **their spies** like sons and **their sons** like foreign spies! Hard to believe? Look at how the representatives (their spies) from China look when they visit our nation; now compare them to their sons (citizenry), forced to work in harsh conditions. If one works hard and keeps their mouth shut, "their social credit" value increases; if they oppose or question the ruling class, all their property and lives are forfeited.

What is the difference between a People's Republic of China Communist and a Union of Soviet Socialist Republics Communist? That depends on whether you count the bodies of the 38 Million who died of famine during the "Great Leap Forward" under the People's Republic of China! And if you believe that the Chinese government was responsible for that famine, it would bring the total to some 73 Million, compared to the Soviet Socialists at 58 Million, making them a bloody second by some 14 Million. Then, to quote Joseph Stalin, **"One death is a tragedy; one million is a *mere* statistic."**

Now I did say *Communist* when a simple reference to Socialist would have done because when the splitting of hairs starts, nobody will say their "socialism" is a death-wish! Over and over, we hear the word-salad responses defending "socialism" when people only mean a few social programs. Even the dictionaries get in on the act and wade into the weeds describing some ideological differences for some classrooms of *intellectual* hoity-toities.

I prefer to let the blood-soaked carnage left behind by those who promised such Utopian deception testify that if the "Road to Hell" were paved, it would be with such promissory intentions!

The following is an overview of Scott Manning's **"Communist Body Count December 4, 2006."** For a detailed break-down of these numbers and historical references, please check this out online... https://scottmanning.com/content/communist-body-count/

- People's Republic of China since 1949:
  73,237,000

- Union of Soviet Socialist Republics 1922-1991: 58,627,000
- Russian Soviet Federated Socialist Republic 1918-1922: 3,284,000
- Democratic People's Republic of Korea since 1948: 3,163,000
- Cambodia 1975-1987: 2,627,000
- Democratic Republic of Afghanistan 1978-1992: 1,750,000
- Vietnam Since 1975: 1,670,000
- People's Democratic Republic of Ethiopia 1974-1991: 1,343,610
- Socialist Federal Republic of Yugoslavia 1945-1992: 1,072,000
- The Chinese Soviet Republic 1931-1934: 700,000
- People's Republic of Mozambique 1975-1990: 700,000
- Socialist Republic of Romania 1947-1989: 435,000
- People's Republic of Bulgaria 1946-1990: 222,000
- People's Republic of Angola 1975-1992: 125,000
- Mongolian People's Republic 1924-1992: 100,000
- People's Socialist Republic of Albania 1946-1991: 100,000
- The Republic of Cuba Since 1961: 73,000
- German Democratic Republic 1949-1990: 70,000
- Socialist Republic of Czechoslovakia 1948-1990: 65,000

- Lao People's Democratic Republic Since 1975: 56,000
- Hungarian People's Republic 1949-1989: 27,000
- People's Republic of Poland 1948-1989: 22,000
- People's Democratic Republic of Yemen 1969-1990: 1,000

So, for those who think that Socialism is just getting a bad rap by all these "statistics," as Joseph Stalin would put it... then I should have stopped at just one tragic death at the hands of a psychopathic Socialist! But if somehow these 150 million deaths aren't worth a guilty verdict, then perhaps billions of future deaths at the hands of the same (as history repeats) should suffice!!

Yet American Socialist/Communists are much more refined with copious amounts of virtue signaling and social justice! It would only take a tragic death of **a known criminal** to have people burn their neighborhoods to the ground in protest and defund their only means of security against those same criminal elements. Causing untold **"statistical" deaths** of children and school-age youths caught in the (gun-free zone) crossfire! The looting, raping, and pillaging by gangs and thugs, all in the name of "just getting some reparations!" Please, spare me the immoral outrage.

Almost 69 years to the day, in a 6-3 decision, the U.S. Supreme Court upheld a New York state law prohibiting communists from teaching in public schools. **And yet Communism seems to be the latest rave in American Universities;**

> "Between 2014 and 2019, Chinese state-owned entities donated at least $315 million to U.S. universities, the Washington Free Beacon found in a recent report. This included an astounding $88 million coming from Chinese contractors and universities that assist the Chinese military in defense research. Approximately 1,000 donations recorded in a Department of Education database revealed that almost 200 CCP-affiliated donors gave to "dozens" of American universities, the Beacon found." (https://spectator.org/ccp-american-universities-confucius-institutes/)

> "Socialism rising: Universities and 'radical' profs helping steer leftward shift in politics, critics say" ...A 2004 poll found that among sociology professors, 25 percent self-identified as "Marxist," 49 percent identified as Democrats, and 5 percent as Republicans. It's not just sociology – in social sciences broadly, more professors identified as Marxist than as conservative..." SOCIALISM Published January 18, 2019 https://www.foxnews.com/politics/socialism-rising-universities-and-radical-profs-helping-steer-leftward-shift-in-politics

My takeaway from the investment by Communist countries into America is that it is the last bastion of free thought in the world and the last hold-out for Capitalism, its main rival. Only Capitalism has pulled more people out of poverty and offers self-determination and prosperity. The tantalizing bribe from Socialism/Communism is equality (not to be confused with equity) with others. However, that is something Western Civilization already offers in spades! Equality to promote one's talents and abilities, with endless examples of those who would be underdogs rising to the top through ambition and hard work.

One would only have to converse with those so-called "equal" souls working in forced labor camps and factories and listen to their stories of promises of prosperity only to live in desperate oppressive poverty. And those who enjoy freedom only do so at the cost of balancing a "social credit system" in sync with their Political overlords.

An unfortunate lock-down in America may have seemed oppressive and the trashing of one's civil rights, but no one had to endure being welded shut in their own homes to survive on what food was present. And yet that too would seem better than a life as a political prisoner enduring forced abortions, forced labor, forced sterility, and forced organ harvesting.

Nothing will wake them from their hypnotic trance if the body count doesn't convince the dreamy-eyed ignorant North American! Previous generations fought against such ideologies on foreign soil, only now to become a civil war dividing our nations. It is a war of the ignorant theorist against the scarred experience of survivors; the previous generations fled those regimes that the current, in full-out lemming run, embrace with open arms!

I feel like we live in privilege, a privilege paid in blood to keep our Nation safe from such depravity and dishonesty. The sheer numbers of these victims of Socialism are too much for the mind to comprehend. Even looking through uncensored pictures of the Holocaust by Nazi Germany, such evil is not conceivable and is almost dismissed.

But dismissed, it is in favor of some alternative narrative featuring free Health Care, forgivable student loans, and "Universal Basic Income." All in the name of "New and Improved Socialism" to take your mind off the bodies in mass graves and the smell of the ovens. Surely our lives must be way more important than those they buried *just five minutes* ago! WE were just a means to an end... our end.

You know that sinking feeling you get, like
we have been drinking the Kool-Aid too
long... and it is time for a reality check?
I hear it all the time; Liberals are inept,
stop with the whole *failed* gov thing—
everyone needs to stop pretending;
the Liberal Government is at war
with Canadian citizens!
All at the behest of
hostile foreign actors
weaponizing our gas prices
mandated medical malfeasance
uncontrolled inflation and regulation;
you can't protest if you can't even eat!
Klaus Schwab brags about penetrating
Trudeau and most of his cabinet
but we are the ones who
end up screwed.
They haven't failed,
they have succeeded in
the ruin of our democracy.
Call 'em what you like, communist,
socialist, even anti-Christ, to be more
accurate but don't call them Canadian!

THE GRAVE RESET

What is so *great* about The *Great* Reset? We are going to take a look at **"8 predictions for the world in 2030"** and take a look at what the World Economic Forum (WEF) is preparing us for:

"8 predictions for the world in 2030"

1) *You'll own nothing. And you'll be happy. Whatever you want you'll rent it'll be delivered by drone*

> **Q:** The World Economic Forum (WEF) just declared that it would facilitate the **theft** of **every person's goods** on planet Earth, and nobody has a problem with that?

2) *The U.S. won't be the world's leading superpower. A handful of countries will dominate*

> **Q:** The World Economic Forum (WEF) If global theft wasn't enough, they also declared it would **facilitate economic war on the USA**, bringing about its financial subservience to a "handful of countries?"

3) *You won't die waiting for an organ donor. We won't transplant organs we'll print new ones instead*

Q: Since the World Economic Forum (WEF) wholly promotes China as the New World *superpower,* won't **"organ printing"** just be code for **organ harvesting?**

4) *You'll eat much less meat. An occasional treat, not a staple for the good of the environment and our health*

Q: Now that we established that the (WEF) plans to 1) take everything you have and force you to rent things like clothes, 2) stop the most prominent voice for human rights on the planet, 3) then use the population as body-part "donors," 4) won't eating anything be an "occasional treat?" ***Beyond meat? Soylent Green*****, anyone?**

5) *A billion people will be displaced by climate change. We'll have to do a better job at welcoming and integrating refugees*

Q: If the **World Economic Forum policies** make heating one's home unaffordable and driving to work impossible, why can't we see that they create chaos that makes a billion refugees?

***6)** Polluters will have to pay to emit carbon dioxide. There will be a global price on carbon; this will help make fossil fuels history*

Q: The World Economic Forum (WEF) has no problem with China leading in CO2 emissions and no ability to stop this pollution giant from continuing; it will only be ***our use*** of fossil fuels that's history?

***7)** You could be preparing to go to Mars Scientists will have worked out how to keep you healthy in space ... a journey to find Alien life?*

Q: The World Economic Forum (WEF) often praises such Earth-depopulation pundits like Bill Gates; are you going to trust these guys with the opportunity to blast you off the earth?

***8)** Western values will have been tested to the breaking point. Checks and balances that underpin our democracies must not be forgotten*

Q: The World Economic Forum (WEF) dares to talk about "Western Values" as they plan to kill, steal and destroy everything that underpins our democracy... WEF? WTF!

> World Economic Forum - February 6, 2017 - 8 predictions for the world in 2030 - This is how our world could change by 2030."
> https://www.facebook.com/worldeconomicforum/videos/10154159674886479 (video)
> **—Ceri Parker, Commissioning Editor,** Agenda, World Economic Forum
> https://www.weforum.org/agenda/2016/11/8-predictions-for-the-world-in-2030/

Do you know how long it takes to get in touch with your Prime Minister? No? How about your Member of Parliament? Don't have a clue? Maybe your Town/City Mayor? No?

Well, for **1)** (in the New World Order), just try and get in touch with the United Nations representative in charge of feeding, clothing, housing, and toilet paper and see how long you are going to "be happy" without owning anything!

And for **2)** *WHO* are you going to call? "**A handful" of communist nations** turning a blind eye to your re-education in some Chinese-Uyghur-style concentration camps... because you complain about not having ***a handful*** of toilet paper?

But don't worry, because for **3)** you won't be dying because you were waiting for an "organ donor"; no, you'll be dying because your organs will be harvested until they can get the "organ printer" back online for the *elites* like Justin Trudeau.

But be of good cheer because **4)** you'll eat much less meat until they can get that "meat" printer back online! It won't matter anyway because you won't be able to afford it.

And best of all, **5)** you too can be among the billions displaced by homelessness caused by **#1)** and **#2)** to teach you a personal lesson on how to welcome and integrate refugees!

6) Good thing "China took the lead" establishing "the right to emit (tons) of CO2, setting the world on a path towards a single carbon price" that only they can afford because they have the whole world buying "Made in China" garbage that has to get replaced in less than a year... if they will *"RENT"* you a replacement! But you won't need that ***gorgeous grill*** anyway, because you won't have any meat to cook!

7) Thank the *lucky* stars we have Mars! "Once we get there, we'll probably discover evidence of alien life" ...a slight twist on the "The Martians are Coming!" by Orson Welles; **we get to go there and scare them with Marxism!!**

At least we can fall back on our education system to teach our present history to future generations; by getting them to remember those antiquated "Western values" that kept Global Marxism at bay for 245 years until it ended with the 45th President of the USA! All because the Communist Globalists took a ***#2*** on the free world, while Canada just stood by and watched as hate for Trump... trumped the love for freedom!

Trump was ***a bull in the China shop***; while bringing back manufacturing, energy independence to America, and tariffs to anyone WHO wanted to shop China, and that is what was needed!

"But Trump was a meanie!" Maybe, but it was evident that he was echoing the voice of anyone on the planet that wanted to stop the Communist Corporate Take-over of Earth! By strengthening America, every other nation followed suit, to the anger of **only** those who wanted to dissolve our sovereignty. Did Trump make mistakes? Sure, one of which was fast-tracking an experimental gene therapy "vaccine!" Don't worry; they can print you up some new genetics, or maybe we can all ***just identify* as NON-GMO *Humans*** after we get the shot/shots, boosters 1,2,3, plus upgrades with software and the latest A.I. Firmware!

> "I thought this was supposed to be a conspiracy theory. But here it is, straight

from Trudeau's mouth: The pandemic is the excuse for a "Great Reset" of the world, led by the United Nations. ... **It means more of the UN, and less of Canada.**"—Ezra Levant
https://www.rebelnews.com/ezra_levant_show_november_16_2020

"Great Reset is corporate communism, and it's coming to America - The coronavirus has handed the far left crowd a golden ticket for government takeover" —Cheryl K. Chumley - The Washington Times - January 9, 2021
www.washingtontimes.com/news/2021/jan/9/great-reset-corporate-communism-and-its-coming-ame/

"Delingpole: The Great Reset Is Not a Conspiracy Theory - Just as the devil's greatest trick was to persuade the world he didn't exist, so it suits promoters of the Great Reset for people to believe they're not serious about their plan — even despite the fact that every last detail is spelled out on the World Economic Forum's website."
—James Delingpole, 20 Nov 2020
https://www.breitbart.com/europe/2020/11/20/the-great-reset-is-not-a-conspiracy-theory/

"COVID-19" was long pre-planned in documents and simulation exercises emanating from the eugenicist Bill Gates

> and the Rockefeller Foundation. A platform with 200 detailed levels is provided by the World Economic Forum led by Klaus Schwab..." —**Weaver, 2 Nov 2020** https://tapnewswire.com/2020/11/the-great-reset-is-global-communism/

Here is where the *"normal"* cuss and swear!

Are these the lifestyles of the "rich and famous?" is Justin Trudeau going to give up all his possessions? How much in advance do I have to order some ***rental*** **underwear** for my kids? will **Klaus Schwab** send his ***Nazi-uber-tank*** around to make sure I get to work on time, or do I have to crawl?

> "**New York, USA, 13 June 2019** – The World Economic Forum and the United Nations signed today a Strategic Partnership Framework outlining areas of cooperation to deepen institutional engagement and jointly **accelerate** the implementation of the **2030 Agenda** for Sustainable Development..."https://www.weforum.org/press/2019/06/world-economic-forum-and-un-sign-strategic-partnership-framework

WORLD ECONOMIC FÜHRER

The "END GAME" is totalitarian Marxism. Offering the "free cheese" in the largest economic mouse trap ever devised (for context, watch An American Tail: Fievel Goes West); these Globalists dry-up resources, create chaos, incite violence and race-bait hungry lawless masses to enslave the compliant and loose the criminals to realize their New World Order. By destroying the middle class, they destroy any hope of the lower class from achieving independence and prosperity apart from the government. By 2030, as Klaus Schwab puts it, **"You Will Own Nothing and Be Happy."**

> **"You Will Own Nothing and Be Happy," Klaus Schwab** ...Founder and Executive Chairman of the World Economic Forum. As Anthony P. Mueller, a professor of economics, warns, "The main thrust of the forum is global control. ... Individual liberty and private property are to disappear from this planet by 2030."
> —Karen Schoen
> https://www.americaoutloud.com/you-will-own-nothing-and-be-happy-klaus-schwab/

People always say that Justin Trudeau is a failure, and I have said it myself, but we couldn't be further from the truth! We are caught up in the emotion of how Trudeau is destroying our nation, while that is just what the NWO has in store for all countries! If one looks at his decisions from a Globalist perspective, it would seem he is a success!

In the previous chapter, we took a look at the WEF "**8 predictions for the world in 2030**." When comparing those "predictions" to Karl Marx's Communist Manifesto, you find an eerie similarity. All the 10 Planks of the Manifesto can be summed up in this first "prediction!" After removing private ownership, all that follows will be inevitable!

And the idea that everything gets delivered by drone indicates that they plan to have everyone in a perpetual lock-down scenario at their every whim and *scariant* variant! The World Economic Forum has declared war on the USA economy, a war that is now being surrendered to by those controlling our government to secure their seats in the "New World Order." As all "counties" get dissolved under a border-less New World Order, then just WHO will be these "HANDFUL" dominating the world?

> Oligarchy: "Oligarchy is a form of government in which a small group of people hold most or all political power."
> https://www.nationalgeographic.org/encyclopedia/oligarchy/

Do people think that the Marxist countries today represent their nations? Is it conceivable that the citizens of these nations are *willingly* trampled for the evil conspiracies of their dictators? Or is it that these corrupt sociopaths that control these nations appeal to the dregs of their societies to get them to enforce their dictates. What would these scummy little creatures be without their traitorous thugs?

Patriotism isn't allegiance to the powers that happen to infiltrate and sabotage our way of governance; it is supposed to be an allegiance to the citizen and constitution while upholding the Charter of Rights and Freedoms!

These parasites take up lodging on a host of political welfare and pollute the very bathwater from which they all drink. Their promises seem pretty cordial, and their goals are quite lofty, but growling and salivation for power and consumption are under their fleece! Like testing an echo chamber, they bounce ideologies off each other until the very sounds they get back are compatible with the detestable grunts they vomit.

These hyenas merely lack opportunity, but once they have it, the fangs of their lust sink deep into the throats that lauded their ascension to seats of power and corruption. Like Nazi Germany, the same working-class people had no thoughts of "taking over the world" ...no more than the average Chinese patriot has today! Does the world even imagine that the average citizen of China stays awake at night dreaming of how much better their life would be if only their dictators had more power? Is it even imaginable that the sweat-shop worker in China dreams of more companies assisting Nike production?

Could it be true that patriotic souls of China dream of a day when they too can be slaves to a New World Order? Where they continue to "own nothing and are *happy*" ...or else? No! They have a gun to their heads and will comply as we will or die.

Death doesn't seem so bad after all when put that way. One could look forward to the end of their part in supporting such a plague on humanity. One might even be excited about deliverance from such oppression and filth. After all, the final destination of mankind has a promise of a certain judgment and equality before an impartial "cloud of witnesses." It is sad that the reality of populations willing to risk death to escape their national prison flee West; if founding Western society values were so bad, there would be an exodus East.

How does this make these political parasites feel? Angry by their Wolfen viciousness! They fear their populations; counting sheep, so many sheep, so very many sheep... they can only lose sleep!

These Globalists have dreams too, you know. They dream of a day that they will only have the compliant to govern. Those who haply follow their dictates like robots, building robots; to populate a world with those who "own nothing and are happy" to serve in **their Utopia**. Not "our" utopia! A place where one cannot buy or sell unless one swears allegiance to their *god!* The one thing they just cannot stand about humans is their humanity.

They would rather a population of programmable "autonomy" governed by "*artificial* intelligence" ...because real intelligence won't and can't stand this kind of bullshit! Well, at least "You won't die waiting for an organ donor" ...because robots don't need organs!

Some people don't like God because He has rules; well, His rules only empower and preserve the dignity of humanity. In a world where people should have only one Sovereign and learn to live in equality, under law and order, one might be wondering where He is. What with all this evil so prevalent in the world today; after removing God from almost every facet of society... except blame; it seems pretty apparent where He is... it seems He is leaving everyone ***"the Hell alone!"***

People have thrown off God like an old garment and use the Name of Jesus Christ as profanity. Many seem only to live to take advantage of another instead of loving their neighbors as themselves. Could it be that God is only allowing us to swim in a larger "Shark tank?" Please don't be angry at God for what people are doing, just given their character and a revealing opportunity.

As to the "innocent," they understand that they will one day meet their maker. They are smart enough to realize that everyone dies and would rather be decent human beings and go the way of those before them, defending truth and justice. Regardless of seemingly outdated ideals, these look to Heaven to be Heaven — Earth to be Earth, and Hell to be the final resting place of the Devil and his messengers! That day can't come soon enough.

GLOBALIST CITIZEN

One might rethink that kind of venture now that Covid craziness has hardly separated us from Marxist-ruled countries, but my question "why" is still on the table... Why does the world see the West as a beacon of hope and freedom? What is it about North America that compels people to leave their homeland and risk illegal entry into Canada or the USA? Why does the world see the West as a beacon of hope and freedom? IF it ever did, it soon won't. Nations exist to separate us democratically from the tyranny of totalitarian governance or colonial serfdom, where we become faceless and mere commodities. **A global village?**

> I foresee a voiceless, mindless mass of enslaved, fearfully complying survivors.

The state of the national heritage of democracy separates us (theoretically) from the many nations dominated by tyrants, where people can't look to protect such things as "Constitutional Rights and Freedoms." Yet more and more, our rights are eroded by the demands of the "Emergency State" that runs roughshod globally over any Nation. Any Government or group that appeals to their sovereignty soon is met with political mandates, media misinformation, Pharma Police, and community lockdowns!

IF we had a voice locally, provincially, or even nationally... how would we think for a moment that our voice could be heard among the 7.5 Billion clamoring for their rights to be heard and met?

Even individuals need boundaries to protect them from the encroachment of abuse, unreasonable demands, or lawless behavior, and why we have walls in our homes, fences in our yards, and curtains on our windows. What seems obvious to the practical individual seems lost on the border-less and nation-less Globalist selling us a new Global ID. Yet because many aren't "buying" that product fast enough, the 'powers that be' are ramping up the purchase by destroying all that we Canadians hold dear. Maybe we would see our need for that "electric car" if gas (let's say) was priced out of reach? It seems "they" are always on time with a new antidote for each crisis introduced.

I was just talking to someone today about a 'conspiracy theory about the disappearance of the "seasonal flu." I suggested that the flu narrative comes around each year, that Big Pharma drums up their best three variant vaccines to save us all from the onslaught. However, I noticed that there wasn't any flu or shots to conquer them in the last few 'Covid years.' They say it is because everyone did such a good job "washing their hands" that we didn't get many colds or the flu, yet that logic seemed to be lost on the Covid variants because they seem to be running full tilt! **IF the Flu were annihilated with hand sanitizer**, Covid would have suffered the same fate!

So, I deduced, that Big Pharma introduces the flu each year through their "vaccines" (upon a "seasonally" conditioned and expectant population). By continuing a pandemic state of emergency with a vaccine-variant to keep "Covid" front and center; perpetuating a sort of Pharma-Coup over sovereign nations and sovereign people's rights by mandating through force, scheduled shots keep us dependent.

You see, *Old Britannia* never got over the *"Independence Day"* from **their** tyrannical reign… so they bypassed our laws, rights, freedoms, and Constitutions; by introducing a scare that would have us all running from our freedoms into the hands of our conspirators! But that's just my theory among thousands of thinking, calculating, and concluding souls, having a good grasp on history and a fair appraisal of the current players in the World Economic Forum!

See what I did there? I used my *free* speech.

A thinking person can now take what I have said, analyze it, and draw conclusions. I fully trust that both those who agree and those who disagree are equally fitted to finding the truth, whether it eventually agrees or disagrees with my statements. It's called discussion, debate, investigation, and the essential information process. Without such an exchange of ideas, we are merely drones of a controlling force rendering us ***serfs*** and pawns in someone else's game… even God doesn't do that! Though He is all-powerful, he allows the ignorant and the informed to choose their course of action and choice, be they rebellious or in agreement.

Considering those who would want to *play* God…

> "In the event that I am reincarnated, I would like to return as a deadly virus, to contribute something to solving overpopulation." —**Duke of Edinburgh**, Prince Philip (10 June 1921 - 9 April 2021)

They say that Prince Philip didn't die of COVID because that would be an ironic conclusion for such people who would enjoy unleashing such indiscriminate pain and suffering on Earth by a deadly virus. Instead of sharing their untold wealth to feed and educate such masses, they would rather kill people than lead them. These are the sentiments of people on their way to their final hopeless destination in the abyss!

Thank God the great Judge isn't an endless regurgitation of their ideals planning humanity's doom! Think about it, their only hope, as they face the final judgment from God, is to be "reincarnated" as a death blow to civilization? What a sad commentary on their momentary gold-plated existence in this life.

What a pathetic summary of *Royal Majesty* and worldly wealth! And these such indictments are hardly rare among the Globalist "elites"; many are they that would want to play God on their way to eternal Hell and damnation. Too harsh? Their grasp on our future and the ideals they force on those *lesser* on the food chain; earn them such *pleasantries* that can hardly suit the destruction, death, and deception they have already accomplished. The wages of their "sin" grant them a far superior judgment by sheer collateral fallout and carnage. These are they that create chaos, only to appear at a late moment to offer some "return to normal" instead of a return to law and order!

> "When you therefore shall see the **abomination of desolation**, spoken of by Daniel the prophet, stand in the holy place, (whoso reads, let them understand:)... For then shall be great tribulation, such as was not since the beginning of the world to this time,

> no, nor ever shall be. And except those days should be shortened, there should no flesh be saved: but for the elect's sake those days shall be shortened. Then if any man shall say unto you, Lo, here is Christ, or there; believe it not. For there shall arise false Christs, and false prophets, and shall show great signs and wonders; insomuch that, if it were possible, they shall deceive the very elect. Behold, I have told you before." —**Jesus of Nazareth**
> (Matthew 24:15; 21-25)

This world is already accepting the forced idea of a One World Government and New World Order, with a One World Dictator acting as *god* (the abomination of desolation); that group currently reigns over Earth's nations and governments! Under the United Nations, each country is now giving up its blood-bought sovereignty to the historical colonizing evils that first enslaved them!

YES, the time is now upon us where this bloodthirsty lot not only desires our political allegiance but our very physical, financial, and spiritual dues! It is not merely good enough for them to claim our physical enslavement but will not stop until we surrender our very souls!

This is nothing new; it was merely months and years from the world's engulfing flood of Noah that this sort tossed off God and decided to make a "name" for themselves by building a "tower to heaven" in Babel. Thousands of years later, they have accomplished the unifications of the same languages and nations to which God scattered them! As back then, they are about to unleash wickedness that would grieve the very hearts of humanity and God, their Creator!

God is all about our freedom to self-defining accomplishment, but mankind was never meant to be a *god* having dominion over their fellows; mankind was only meant to have dominion and management over their world and resources.

Answer me this: which totalitarian government has ever cared for and loved its people? Have not they forced, enslaved, and starved their weak or obstinate citizens? Freedom isn't a mandated existence; it is the same lifestyle that those on top enjoy, down to those on the bottom. But that is not what they offer. Love is not what they offer. Robotic trans-humanism is what they offer. It is where you surrender your will for the "common good" ...a "good" that they get to redefine their productive bottom line to sustain their resources, not sustainable ones. This will be the realization of Marxism as true Darwinism, the survival of the stronger at the expense of the weaker.

Am I to offer some comfort? Sure, but it comes in the way of a question of choice, a red pill instead of the blue. Does it seem more feasible that George Orwell was some doomsday prophet of a dystopial future, or was **this Eric Blair (Orwell's actual name)** part of a secret society following a blueprint for a New World Order and the failure of Democracy? The planned loss of democracy is the only thing that separates us from barbaric totalitarian dominance and disparate survival.

The book is referred to as **1984**, supposedly futuristic science fiction by the English novelist George Orwell. Or it was a peek into the heart of collaborating secret societies he belonged to that would ensure global tyranny.

Interestingly, George Orwell of the **Fabian Society** (with the logo as a wolf in sheep's clothing); in discourse with a former French teacher at Eton College (Aldous Huxley); curiously sent a letter to Orwell stating: "there may be a large-scale biological war" ...to bring about this kind of global change to society.

Now in the face of the COVID pandemic and Great Reset "opportunity" waged on the entire world, Orwell was privy to the inevitable plans of such a secret society or society with secrets... or he was reading the book of Revelation?

The Greek word "pharmakeia" is used in the scriptures as "sorcery" in English; it's where we get the word *pharma*.

> "And the light of a candle shall shine no more at all in thee; and the voice of the bridegroom and of the bride shall be heard no more at all in thee: for thy merchants were the great men of the earth; for by your *pharmakeia* were all nations deceived." —Revelation 18:23

Now the illustrious Fabian Society was founded in 1884, and *coincidentally* Orwell named his novel 1984 a mere 100 years to accomplish this fall of humanity. It would seem these plans were somewhat prematurely optimistic on the part of the society members or held back by some force greater than the whims of men in secret rooms.

Much like the present-day "Agenda 21 and Agenda 2030" ultimately calling for the "Depopulation Of 95% Of the World By 2030", we who are alive today will see whether or not they can pull it off!

These UN Agendas seem to be a page from Orwell's 1984, but don't kid yourself; the manifestation of global secret societies has fine-tuned their criminality to make the Fabian Society seem quaint or practically *old-school*.

'George Orwell' quotes fitting for today:

> "A people that elect corrupt politicians, imposters, thieves, and traitors are not victims, but accomplices."

> "Power is not a means; it is an end. One does not establish a dictatorship in order to safeguard a revolution, one makes the revolution in order to establish the dictatorship."

> "In a time of deceit telling the truth is a revolutionary act."

> "Looking at the whole world as a whole, the drift for many decades has been not towards anarchy but towards the reimposition of slavery."

> "What is needed is the right to print what one believes to be true, without having to fear bullying or blackmail from any side."

> "No one can get up much enthusiasm for a Government which puts you in jail if you open your mouth."

> "The choice for mankind lies between freedom and happiness and for the great bulk of mankind, happiness is better."

> "We know that no one ever seizes power with the intention of relinquishing it."

CIVIL DESTRUCTION

Today, I have to tell you that I sat in front of my keyboard with my head in my hands, wondering why. With all the voices of reason out there that oppose the Communist takeover of Canada, why would I need to write another book on the subject?

With the ***Rebel.Media, TNC.News*** and many other patriotic journalists fighting for our freedoms, why would I need to put my face out there? As an insignificant blogger and novice book writer with an (unpaid) ministry background, why would I jeopardize any outreach on such a divisive topic? Especially when people are lined up and down every street in Canada protesting this Globalist Coup on our Democracy? Because I need to be one of them. WE all need to be counted among them!

I told my wife of my doubts, wondering if I could make so much a ripple in the *ocean* of disgust that at least half of Canadians feel they are starting to wake up to this tyranny on our ballot. Faking another lockdown just in time for an election? While most of the world is tossing off the *plandemic* restrictions? I said I felt as though I were unarmed in this battle of wits and strategy. With no creds but the patriotism that pulses through my veins, I sense an overwhelming drive to have my voice sing in chorus with the millions of other dissenters to this hostile foreign invasion.

Why would I need to mount a cheering section with all the voices in battle? What do I have that will be heard above neighbors' clapping and yelling for more Communism?

Is that a bit too much?

Let me tell you; I was buying some cupboards from a friend who, when asked about this kind of "communism," as I put it, exclaimed, "I am a communist!" I was astonished by his come-back! Here is the guy that owns lots of land and equipment and seeks to develop more, yet paradoxically he is for higher carbon taxation and less "greed," as he self-loathingly puts it. He wants tighter lockdowns and forced health orders to stop the spread of *COVID*, not knowing that these kinds of measures are the virus!

Wow. I am not saying that the "COVID" bug isn't real; I am saying that the unprecedented hostile takeover of our freedoms is political theater to scare the population into accepting a full-on Dictatorship! It is designed to alleviate the fears *cooked up* in labs and boardrooms that own the patents on these diseases and their "vaccinations" and gene therapies to garner more control and fear. Just putting it that way, I sense an inspiration to mount an all-out verbal assault, standing with those who pay the price daily for my freedom from such ignorance.

Though battling beside those better armed and better educated may seem like carrying a slingshot into battle, don't kid yourself; even those credentialed and acclaimed sounding similar alarms are also dismissed. **"The Great Barrington Declaration"** features thousands and thousands of top scientists and medical professionals who would like a measured approach and focused protection of those affected by ***GOVID-19***. Here is just an into on their website:

> "The Great Barrington Declaration... Coming from both the left and right, and around the world, we have devoted our careers to protecting people. Current lockdown policies are producing devastating effects on short and long-term public health. The results (to name a few) include lower childhood vaccination rates, worsening cardiovascular disease outcomes, fewer cancer screenings and deteriorating mental health – leading to greater excess mortality in years to come, with the working class and younger members of society carrying the heaviest burden. Keeping students out of school is a grave injustice." https://gbdeclaration.org/

If the public isn't willing to accept an experts' word, they won't be willing to take the "anecdotal" testimony and concern from those directly affected by *COVID* and its Communism. Last year's conspiracy theory of "CO" (Corona) "V" (Virus) ID (Identification) has now become *"old news"* as the plandemic became the catalyst for a **Global ID** to be mandated on the entire world... **all in the name of health care/national security!**

So, I go to war. I am armed with a keyboard and the ability to publish my books. Effective? Only time will tell. One thing is for sure; it will be clear where I stood on these issues and how History will judge me. I care less where or how I die, by public "cancellation" or guillotine... the fact is I am going to die. And die I will, along with those who would be my enemies. We will all stand before our Creator; only time will separate that inevitability.

While reading **TheAtlantic.com** online magazine:

"World War II: The Holocaust"
https://www.theatlantic.com/photo/2011/10/world-war-ii-the-holocaust/100170/

...I noticed a curious thing, both those killed in the Holocaust and those who killed them, are, by now, both gone to see their Maker.

Both sets of bones are buried and soon to be dust or ashes. **My question is simple: What did it profit those holding the guns above those shot? Both are now dead?** The difference is how History records their choices and their final testimony. Mass graves or fancy coffins? Crematorium or Nazi ovens? Like those burned at the stake by those who lit the match, an indelible record in history: courageous or coward!

Surely those Germans had the same warnings we have today, those private citizens who announced their disapproval of the demonization of half the population who were only asking questions. For us to question and receive with a level of skepticism the governmental lockdowns, questioning our government's allegiance to other global dictators, should seem only rational. But it is met with...

"You just want to kill Grandma!"

IF Canada cannot see that quarantining the sick instead of the healthy is reasonable and protecting the vulnerable by letting the healthy work to support by taxes those who could care for them, they have swallowed a pill from which they cannot recover! Until they get fed to mass graves or furnaces, the bodies of 150 million killed under Socialism can't be wrong!

If we want to know how this happened in Germany, just look in the mirror!

It baffles me that daily our Members of Parliament can stand and spill their guts of breaches to our National Security, ethics violations, outright bribery in campaign violations, even Trudeau Trust fund donations by the Chinese, and all we get from our Military and RCMP is crickets?

Either they are complaisant in this ***Global GOVID Coup,*** or they are involved! Just like the Gestapo rising through the ranks of the Nazi Police, there will be those with ambitions who will take their rightful places among the RCMP and Military to enforce ANY measure these Globalists instruct.

After all, they are just "doing their job" and have families to feed!

These "public servants" were never intended to be voted in to be our Leaders or our Dictators. But they have become what they were groomed to be. When you can see that Justin Trudeau's father was a communist, and his greatest admiration was for other communists, it is no wonder that Justin's aspirations and actions follow that ideology. It isn't the ideological communism that is being realized, the kind where everyone is equal—No! It is the bait and switch of political deception where the free cheese is bait for the proverbial mousetrap!

SOCIALIST JUSTICE WARRIOR

What is Justice? Is it equality? What is equality? You don't need to look very far to see that many people differ on those terms alone without defining morality's mechanism. Morality? What is that? See how that can be a problem; things aren't as straight forward as most think. Some would say all we need is a little "common sense!" But is it that common? In what seems a world tossed into a post-logic mindset... ***♪ it is beginning to look a lot like CRISIS! ♪*** For this reason, we have documents such as constitutions and the Bill of Rights or Charters of Freedom; they were drafted for times such as these.

For instance, in the Kyle Rittenhouse trial: the verdict didn't have much consequence when many people had made up their minds long before the jury gave their summary. **The media drove the narrative** that this young boy from Kenosha, Wisconsin (who shot three people in self-defense) was a "white supremacist" vigilante out for blood, and he got it! Joe Biden started that ball rolling even before he was President. Still, it is hard to see where one lie ends and another begins. *Big Media* generates chaos-causing confusion, and its outcome is always the same, **unrest on the streets and more government control**.

If one just stands back and looks at the context of such media movies, their protagonists and antagonists, the villains and the nobles are more like the good-ole'-days of serfdom where it is more a class struggle than a race war! If the "Noble" elites can pit the lower (nonpolitical) class against their peers and keep them fighting amongst themselves, they will be clueless about the ground shifting under their feet. Kyle Rittenhouse defends his right of presumption of innocence until a jury of his peers is proven guilty. But a mob bent on a political outcome has little to do with justice. The lives lost or the precedence in such a trial bears on the inalienable right to self-defense!

And yet the mainstream media somehow paints a 17-year-old Kyle Rittenhouse as a ***vigilante*** poster boy?!

> **Definition of vigilante**
> : a member of a volunteer committee organized to suppress and punish crime summarily (as when the processes of law are viewed as inadequate)
> broadly: a self-appointed doer of justice
> www.merriam-webster.com/dictionary/vigilante

Now there's an example of mass hypnotism at its best; one finds a way to see past the forest fire, the trees, bushes, shrubs, and fruit trees... all to pick out a lone sunflower plant and condemn it for contributing to *"the greenhouse effect!"* **All the rioters, looters, and murderers unleashed in various cities under the BLM banner** (just to name one) were by definition vigilantes, and yet one person there to support his family and friends against such a murderous mob (with an established reputation); is seen as the antagonist and as the vigilante? Smh! I don't know about you, but when I hear the word "vigilante" (thanks to the Media), all I can see is a "white guy" out for his kind of justice. And yet the stats are quite the opposite…

> **George Floyd Riots Caused Record-Setting $2 Billion in Damage, New Report Says. Here's Why the True Cost Is Even Higher**
> https://fee.org/articles/george-floyd-riots-caused-record-setting-2-billion-in-damage-new-report-says-here-s-why-the-true-cost-is-even-higher/

> **Thousands of cops were injured, over $2 billion in damage during Floyd riots. Where are the "congressional hearings"?**
> https://www.lawenforcementtoday.com/thousands-of-cops-were-injured-over-2-billion-in-damage-during-floyd-riots-where-are-the-congressional-hearings/

> **Murder Rates Spike 30% — Biggest Increase on Record…**it appears likely

> that increased murder rates are due to highly publicized efforts to "Defund the Police" and unconstitutional coronavirus lockdowns. "The Democrats' celebration of violent riots in cities across the United States throughout 2020, and complete abandonment of law and order and lack of support for the brave men and women in law enforcement has had horrific consequences,"
> https://headlineusa.com/murder-rates-spike-30-biggest-increase-on-record/

I am not asking anyone to "talk" about their "take" on the BLM Riots or the devastating impacts on the Black neighborhoods they claim to represent, nor the white-supremacist infiltration among this BLM vigilante group to further promote and drive such chaos in every Black community in America. **I am only asking you to think about it.**

Say what you want about mob justice; it wasn't accomplished for George Floyd. Period. The opposite was achieved, and every riot leading to murderous vandalism and looting has only hurt struggling Black communities. It isn't "justice"; it's a plan to target certain communities by race-baiting and a Globalist Media bent on a New World Order.

Nicholas Sandmann was another media-mob injustice; he too was a young white man painted as *"paleface"* only out to destroy Native Peoples and their land rights. Yet when the dust had settled, the Media had to *settle* on a 250Million dollar defamation lawsuit!

The same will pan out for Kyle Rittenhouse. The "target" isn't those that get socially canceled, but rather the neighborhoods driven as a mob by the George Soros and the **Klaus Schwab** types. These do the bidding of a faceless Crimeopoly funding it all. How long will we be content to sacrifice the little "sunflowers" standing up for their God-given rights in the face of this Godless globalist construct?

Notice how I didn't say "(g)odless" ...because these and all major merchants of Earth *would be* and want to play "god" with the lives of the peasantry. Their soldiers are the mercenaries that hold no patriotism but for the dollar and determination of their puppet masters. They employ those who are the antithesis of "for love of God and Country" ...criminals in every respect.

Look at those Rittenhouse *extinguished*; they were actually white-supremacist scum that rioted, looted, and burned down Black neighborhoods; a white criminal child rapist, domestic criminal abuser, and home invader. These are the media darlings! What the actual ___?! And what about the criminals rioting, looting, and burning down their own neighborhoods? For a pair of Nikes?

"The Independent Falsely Stated Rittenhouse Shot 3 Black Men

The Independent falsely claimed that Kyle Rittenhouse shot three black men after he was acquitted of all charges Friday for shooting three white men in self-defense during the August 2020 Kenosha, Wisconsin, riots..."

https://www.msn.com/en-us/news/us/the-independent-falsely-stated-rittenhouse-shot-3-black-men/ar-AAQVzsG

MSNBC's Tiffany Cross calls Kyle Rittenhouse "little murderous white supremacist"

https://www.youtube.com/watch?v=I0nuxHtsrxg

10 heinous lies about Kyle Rittenhouse debunked: Devine

"Of all the willful lies and omissions in the media's coverage of the Steele dossier, Brian Sicknick, the Covington kids, Jussie Smollett, the Wuhan lab, Hunter Biden's laptop and so on, nothing beats the evil propaganda peddled about Kyle Rittenhouse." —Miranda Devine

https://nypost.com/2021/11/17/10-debunked-heinous-lies-about-kyle-rittenhouse-devine/

Don't be fooled by the "moral high ground" the Media seems to hold in their condemnation of vigilantism; because it is really the condemnation of any vigilantism outside their ranks!

They alone want to have the *Crimeopoly* on such chaos and the license to kill, maim, destroy and cancel in their brand of mob justice! And when you tally the score at the end of the day, the Black neighborhoods are destroyed and degraded, and what becomes apparent is the revelation of who the real Judas is! Considering specific black news anchors (paid) to vomit this Globalist Agenda, a look down through history reveals a similar sad tragedy by human traffickers who sell out their people!

Who was the actual "white supremacist?" A video of Joseph Rosenbaum, one of the people shot and killed by Kyle Rittenhouse in Kenosha, showed him earlier in the night taunting armed civilians, saying, "Shoot me, n___a." **Did the media run with that?** No, because it is contrary to the attempts to paint Rittenhouse as a "white supremacist" ...when the opposite is true! The media was quick to defame the character of someone publicly vindicated by a video released early in reporting the shooting in Kenosha. And time after time, the mainstream agenda twists a narrative that flows contrary to what everyone can see plainly.

Days after Kyle Rittenhouse got acquitted on all charges, Darrell E. Brooks, 39 (who reportedly had previously used his vehicle as a weapon), ran down and killed five white people. And even though this "rapper" produced a video hating whites, the media seems quite "restrained" when making similar conclusions. Though the footage of the slaughter of paraders seems clearly intentional, the press is doing a *twister-act* to produce a narrative that somehow Brooks was a victim of a domestic dispute and was out of his faculties, somehow rendering him innocent of murder. I am pointing out that the media does not have our best interest or the truth when "reporting" the news.

The mainstream media seems only a tool to cause unrest, so a more sinister agenda can be reached. More chaos equals more federal intervention. Sadly, the media seems only a flamethrower on the kindling of simple minds incited to destroy and tear down a society that has served as the best example of freedom and democracy.

Take the BLM guise as "social justice warriors" ...openly Marxist. This group would see society burned to the ground, law enforcement charred, and innocent businesses that serve black communities torched beyond recovery ...and that is not a White Supremacist agenda?? Who suffers? Who is worse off? How does that help American blacks? It doesn't!

This pseudo-social justice is a *socialist-justice* agenda to disarm and disenfranchise the very people they claim to serve. No different from the Chinese Communist Party preaching about representing the people's labor force while enslaving the same! The overlords in Marxism always **promise** prosperity, but it is only for the compliant stooges of their regime so that any discussion deemed as a dissenting voice will be suffocated under a social-credit score.

The promises are always the same; **the people must do without to achieve the ultimate victory**. This carrot-dangling bait-and-switch only serves the masters of that destiny. **The value of these pawns** is only worth as much as their place in the game as *Socialist Justice Warriors*.

Do you want more social justice? **Vote.**

My advice is simple, vote brains, not hair
...and vote heart, not breasts!

Don't look at the outside facade and mistake it for the inward character. Don't vote based on the traditional norms of your historical political party. Vote for those who are undying patriots and defenders of our Charter of Rights and

Freedoms—laid out in the highest courts we can hold. **And most importantly, vote! Yes, Vote!**

Vote like the future of Canada depends on it! No matter what frauds they use to keep you from it, your voting rights are the first things to go!

Oh, and make sure that **when** you vote, you launch lawsuits against the Government that most assuredly will commit fraud to keep its power.

It could be that the West has had it too good, which is why we are all shocked when these things happen. We have let patriots die, bleed for us, and pray for us for too long. Now we must do our dying, bleeding, and praying. The truth is, we are invested heavily in an Earth that we will too soon leave behind. We must not forget to invest a bit in the legacy we leave for others and a bit for the final judgment that we all will face.

WHO'S YOUR DADDY?

I have been asked if I believe that Justin Trudeau's father was, in reality, Fidel Castro because of some similarities in looks when Castro was younger. I have also been asked if the cover of my book is going too far in possibly mocking the pain of the Prime Ministers' possible upbringing. Some would say that regardless of another man's actions, we have no right to make fun of them or mock their heritage, you know, *"do unto others as you would have them do unto you!"*

On the other hand, some feel that Justin Trudeau has opened this door to ridicule because of his mockery of ethnic groups while going black-face, brown-face, and two-faced! I merely appeal to his sense of political theater.

It wasn't that easy to *photoshop* the **'young Fidel'** to look like **Justin Trudeau**; it took me 5 minutes! Just kidding! I had to remove some weight from the face of Fidel Castro and shrink some of his upper body mass, being that he was definitely a bigger build than Trudeau. But *moistly,* the facial features, the cutting, pasting, morphing... and more cutting, pasting, and morphing!

To be clear, even if we got into the lifestyles of Justin's parents and allegedly whether or not Justin was Fidel Castro's son, I couldn't actually care less. We can be pretty confident that Fidel Castro and Justin Trudeau are related. From all the research I have done plus the Photoshop®, chop and drop... definitely related! I mean... we do have to go as far back as Adam and Eve, but they are definitely related!

Who cares? Does it somehow make a difference whose father a person has? There were times in my childhood I wished for a different father, and my father wished I was someone else's son. My father used to say to his friends that I was *"a son only a mother could love!"* Regardless of how we got into this world, we are here with a purpose, yet not so much with a plan.

Justin shouldn't have a problem with the cover of this book anyway; he could call it **"Castro-face"** and be ready to attend "Triunfo de la Revolucion" on his next visit to Cuba! It wouldn't be that hard; he did pull off *"black & white face"* nicely! He could keep half of his face its natural color (a pale embarrassment red) and go full *"Munsters"* on the other. But all acting aside, his current role as a globalist traitor has the world seriously asking...

"Who owns **LIAR.COM**?"

I can't fault the guy for ***dressing up*** and playing roles he's not fitted for. My family can tell you of the time **(as a child)** I thought that I could be like *"Mary Poppins"* (or at least a close relative), as I climbed up to the top of our roof with an umbrella and jumped off! Maybe this is where I was also inspired to *identify* as Spiderman! Driving my entire family *up the walls* because of my crazy antics! From Evel Knievel to Chuck Norris, accented with some Marvel Comics sprinkled with Happy Days—I played many roles; some say to "escape," while others said to get attention. But I can tell you, growing up in a Northern community, **as much as I wanted to be Native** (and I very much did), **I never went "brown-face!"**

Acting, or in my case "acting out," has been a lifelong trait of mine; even though identifying as myself started at about the age of 15 when I left home, I could see how others would like to carry on such drama into their early 20's. **My point is** if one at the age of 40+ is still playing 'dress up' as part of their political career as Justin is, we should at least honor such dedication with an Emmy Award as they did with *"Killer"* Cuomo!

This serious role-playing doesn't go unnoticed by political powers that need an *actor* to pull off a good heist. Youth trauma survivors like Justin are best suited for such roles; they seem to have all the empathy beaten out of them so they can chameleon any part necessary.

I am not saying that I believe Justin Trudeau is a sociopath and that he ***suffers*** from a dissociative identity disorder. Instead, I think he immensely ***enjoys*** his dissociative identity disorder! It seems this part he gets to play makes him all *gushy* inside, like living on a big movie set; each *"Action!"* is a "long take" towards the "final cut!"

Justin takes acting tips from some real evil world players in his reality TV show, like **George** Soros, ***George*** *Harvey*, **George** Mark *'Moloch'* Brown, Prince Charles Philip Arthur **George**, **George** Bush, plus the not-so-evil **George** of the Jungle. Yes, even **George** of the Jungle!

> "The George of the Jungle cartoons are a send-up of the Tarzan mythos. Square-jawed, dim-witted George is the king of the jungle. Almost every time he tries to swing to the rescue through the trees, he crashes into one, usually while someone else is warning him, "Watch out for that..." WHAM! "...tree!"
> https://tvtropes.org/pmwiki/pmwiki.php/WesternAnimation/GeorgeOfTheJungle

This bumbling-idiot-motif with that wavy hair really makes the girls swoon! Such a lovable dweeb that one cannot resist. Did I mention he is substantially wealthier than he was as a drama teacher? He did have his daddy's millions, but that is nothing compared to the *"back-bathing"* he is getting from China and some Georges!

Did you ever wonder why the Queen of England hasn't done anything about little Justin selling off her Canadian interest to China? Could it be that she is behind the whole merger through some Georges?

IF you ever learned anything from Sun Tzu, it should have been... ***"When you are strong, appear weak."*** WHO is the *weakest*-looking Global player? **Oh, that's right, the Queen.**

Just follow the money... with more than a 6th of the planet's inhabitable land, players like Bill Gates, Jeff Bezos, Elon Musk, or anyone else can't compare to the 33Trillion net worth of **"the Queen's private estate."**

A lesson on "money" ...the more "money" you have, the more you are indebted to the system that created it! You didn't actually think that guys like George Soros had their own money, did you? **Once more:** the more money you have, the more that money has you! If your wealth is determined by *a piece of paper or digital currency,* those who print that paper determine your wealth. They can either value or devalue your net worth based on their political agenda at any particular time. Whose living face or inscription is on the Canadian currency?

[more about **the Queen** in the next chapter]

YES, one day, they will cancel all "debt," but in that same stroke of a pen, they will cancel ALL NET WORTH. Many people used to mock talk about everyone having to get "**the mark of the beast**," ...until now, there has never been a time that an actual one-world government could have been possible!

The mask will be off, and it will become apparent that they alone will determine our "value." It will be clear why we won't have to own anything because we are the *trade-able* commodity. **Are you finding it hard to breathe?** It's not the masks, but the chains they are tightening around our necks!

I could care less about someone's heritage, who their dad is, or their mom is; and I could care even less about their proclivities and orientation. What I do care about is the ability of any individual to carry out the oath they are entrusted with as representatives of Canada, or did they merely promise such patriotism to pander to the people just long enough to place a knife in their backs?!

> "And *(the beast)* causes all, both small and great, rich and poor, free and bond, to receive a mark in their right hand, or in their foreheads: **so that no man might buy or sell, unless he that had the mark**, or the name of the beast, or the number of his name." (Revelation 13:16-17)

> "... **If anyone worship the beast and his image, and receive his mark in his forehead**, or in his hand, The same shall drink of the wine of the wrath of God, which is poured out without mixture into the cup of his indignation; and he shall be tormented with fire and brimstone in the presence of the holy angels, and in the presence of the Lamb: And the smoke of their torment ascends up for ever and ever: and they have no rest day nor night, who worship the beast and his image, and whosoever receives the mark of his name. Here is the **patience** of the saints: here are they that keep the commandments of God, and the faith of Jesus." (Revelation 14:9-12)

All innuendo against Justin Trudeau aside, I believe all evidence proves Justin Trudeau is the son of Pierre and Margaret Trudeau, married on March 4, 1971. Then Christmas Day, December 25, 1971, Justin was born nine months later. Pierre and Margaret Trudeau's first visit to Cuba was in 1976, five years after Justin was born.

Pictures of the visit with Margaret with Fidel Castro have Margaret in a blouse matching their arrival photos at the airport with four-month-old Michel.

> "This Week in History: 1971 PM Pierre Trudeau marries Margaret Sinclair" —John Mackie
> https://vancouversun.com/news/local-news/this-week-in-history-1971-pm-pierre-trudeau-marries-margaret-sinclair/

> "Margaret Trudeau fondly remembers 1976 trip to Cuba and the 'charming' dictator who cuddled her baby" —**Postmedia News**
> https://nationalpost.com/news/canada/margaret-trudeau-fondly-remembers-1976-trip-to-cuba-and-the-charming-dictator-who-cuddled-her-baby

But what about **'Who's your Granddaddy?'** Our current deputy prime minister and minister of finance, **Chrystia Freeland's** "maternal grandfather, is Michael (Mikhailo) Chomiak, a **notorious Nazi collaborator** from the start to the end of WWII. **Many say she is Justin's (WEF) handler.** https://canadianpatriot.org/?s=Chrystia+Freeland

LOVE OF GOD AND COUNTRY

Many of us know a couple of things about Canada's history, wars, or maybe the displacement of indigenous people. The participation in two World Wars defending democracy while holding a contrary part in the residential school's tragedy presents a paradox of back-and-forth on human rights and abuses.

Though Canada had a sanctuary for blacks escaping slavery through the *"underground railroad"* before the Emancipation Proclamation, individuals made that happen, and not so much a Canadian policy. One cannot even attempt to sum up a nation such as ours with "facts" about our history without considering that certain individuals are responsible for more than blanket blame upon all. Equally, we cannot attribute the heroism of certain individuals to what it means to be Canadian.

Ours is a nation struggling to be more than just the sum of its parts; just when Canadians are coming together to right the wrongs and recognize the contributions made to our nation at such a great cost, Globalism comes with only the mere "promise" of utopia. When Canada seems defined by its multiculturalism and diversity; economically independent, rich in resources and potential, **"Globalism" is offered to cure us of our "oppression" and victim status** as individuals apparently without representation. Really? This nation provides the greatest known opportunity for advancement in the world... and somehow, we need a global government to lick our wounds? It's more like licking its chops!

Any abuses perpetrated on serfs by all-powerful entities owning everything will get silenced as they do now in China. We have problems, alright, but our most prominent is the intervention of "upper class" ...elites manipulating our media, education, and work environment. All to brainwash us into a dream where we "will all own nothing, and we will be happy."

My question is, who will control those things we now own? Our personal property, achievements, and investments? I will tell you, a heartless, faceless entity that will **certainly not be accountable to those who have nothing and are incapable of representing themselves before a "world court."** All because Canadians lazily refuse to educate themselves on their rights to defend their heritage!

For the Love of God —and Country

"We do need to learn our history, and there is much to be proud of. I'm grateful to be a

> part of a nation which has done and is doing some great things in the world. But let's not fool ourselves: **we are not God's chosen nation**, and our history is as agonizing and terrible as it is great."
> https://www.huffpost.com/entry/for-the-love-of-god-and-c_b_3491123

We may not be *"**God's Chosen Nation,**"* but if anyone reads the **Canadian Charter of Rights and Freedoms**, they will find in the very **first** words **we are a nation that chose God!**

*"Whereas **Canada is founded upon principles that recognize the supremacy of God** and the rule of law"*
https://laws-lois.justice.gc.ca/eng/const/page-12.html

In Part 1 of the Constitution Act (1982), you find that **Canada** isn't merely resources and political power; real people build futures in a struggle to pursue happiness, purpose, and free thought! These battles are fundamental in a civil society exchanging differing world views and challenging each other to consider those opposing forces that educate us.

Our constant exploration of diversity actually ratifies our purest motives and sheds us of our hypocrisy; living in a free world, free to act and face the legal consequences of such actions, is what it means to be a law-abiding Canadian. As for those who desire only to be parasitic on the backs of such heritage, my only hope is that their eyes are open to their full potential before it's too late.

Five minutes ago, racism was becoming a thing of the past ...now (according to them), people born white; are naturally racist! One would never define a nation's citizenry by their political mascot, no more than they would judge an individual by their skin color or family history.

That is precisely what this "New World Order" is offering; freedom to express racism, bigotry, and every other evil intent... as long as it is media-friendly! Only six corporations control what we are supposed to accept as being palatable. As long as our *vice* is directed **at those they target for political reasons**, it is protected!

These Global elites and money-changers of our society are the ones who profit from our chaos. They finance both sides of our struggles, providing enough instability for us to go into debt to overcome these adversities while delivering a government "solution" to a problem they created!

We finance their endeavors of creating problems they alone can fix, keeping us in fear of a *bogeyman* that is always only a step away from eating our lunch while dangling the "carrot" of security to keep us from said bogeyman! Mankind has always traded its freedoms for security, but when things get so bad that people no longer fear... and are no longer manipulated... they punish the traitors that sold out their nation!

Do people actually think that Justin Trudeau represents Canada? That Joe Biden represents the United States of America? Or that Xi Jinping truly represents China? That's a hard No!

Do the people of Canada want to buy oil from Saudi Arabia when they have their own natural resources developed in Alberta? Not to mention anything of the other provinces that equally sit on their oil reserves?

Is it rational to assume that citizens of our nation favor the sell-off of our mining to China? Our food production and farmland to China? And amounts of unpayable debt to China? Or the training of China's troops for "Cold Weather" warfare that could easily be used against our country? What about sharing our nation's technology and national security to China through a Belt and Road Initiative *lobbying* (better known as bribery); ...**did Canadians vote for that?**

On the flip side, did the average Chinese citizen want to be a part of a *"Nazi-China"* takeover of the world? Did they want to put their children in harm's way to fulfill a heartless dictator's ambition? Did they vote to have their children, parents, and relatives' servants of the State to build this globalist take-over? Will they share in the plunder of all the confiscated goods by these resurrected ghastly regimes? Oh, that's right, they will be too happy "owning nothing!"

They promise to rob from the rich—**but rob from everyone equally** to keep them at the same poverty level, **advancing only those friends of the State!** Socialism is a lie, a poor promise without its very fulfillment.

Xi Jinping *sings songs* about his years "among the people," but his actions spit in their faces and enslave his nation's children. They come out in droves, waving flags and cheering to high heaven... **with a gun to their heads!**

Do you think those who show up in uniform do so out of their own volition, or do you think that back home, they have secret police monitoring their family's thoughts and actions to see if they are loyal to the Chinese Communist Party (CCP)? These *dedicated* soldiers will do what they are told when they are told to do it, even if it means targeting their own family and friends. Because there is only one family, only one friend, and only one *god*... the party, the CCP!

Do Canadians want that " investment " to control our nation's policies? Do Canadians want to identify as a distribution center for Global Communism? Sound harsh? What will Canada look like when we have to trade the control of our lands and resources to those financing our debt? The debt they created by unleashing a bio-weapon upon the world as a crisis that only they and their cronies could fix!

We cannot be naive to think that during economic warfare with Trump's USA (while China was losing big-time), China didn't drop this Covid bio-bomb to level the playing field.

They say desperate times call for desperate measures; even Nazi Germany was trying to cook up bio-weapons by experimenting on captives to unleash upon their enemies. **Yet somehow, the Chinese Communist Party is so morally above that?** "Surely the CCP wouldn't sacrifice their own people to gain a global advantage?"

Xi Jinping, who worships Mao Zedong (Chairman of that same Communist Party of China), did just that! And it worked! The popular physiological propaganda against the reality of tyrannical atrocities focuses on heroes because those admired for wading into the kill zone, take the focus off the ones who hatched these morbid schemes to begin with.

Pretty soon, Canada will have no choice as our "representatives" sell off or give away for personal favors, our nation, and the control of its resources. We, too, will have to show up cheering and waving the flag of *Chinada* if we want food for our children, clothes for our backs, and the ability to move freely through "our" nation.

Who would have thought that China could declare war on the world with impunity? They dropped a viral bomb, and the globalists cheered? Why? Because the fearful will easily trade all their freedoms for security. They will take experimental shots that may have a long-lasting sickness that only Big Pharma can treat. And take on massive debts that only Big Money can finance. By believing a lie, only Big Media can sustain!

Did you ever wonder why every time a crisis is logically analyzed, it's found to be manipulated by our governments, stripping us of our wealth and freedoms? Like the flooding in China at this time, though it was the government's negligence not to reinforce and rebuild failing water dams, the narrative gets muddied by talk of "Climate Change," and heroic first responders... as millions are displaced and thousands are dead. The media diversion response is that "health care workers are such heroes" for being on the frontline of a pandemic ...of their creation! It is a media manipulation to silence governmental blame.

Somehow if you ask how governments can put their people in jeopardy, kill their citizens by their negligence and treat them like experimental lab rats, you are the one that is not patriotic. You are the one not supportive of first responders and those giving their lives to help in times of the very trouble they created and perpetrated this on an unsuspecting citizenry!

They are good at creating a crisis so big that the people are left to say stuff like, *"Who cares who is to blame? We just need to pull together!"* And it works time after time; we are conditioned to run into the burning buildings, the line of fire, and the raging torrents... all because of those orchestrating these elaborate "Hunger Games!"

These times of crisis are guns to our heads, and the threats to our families are an axe to our futures. These keep us wearing masks, locking ourselves in our houses and towns, and taking dangerous experimental shots that can permanently damage our health and make us dependent on treatments only "they" can provide. Why? Because to question where the trouble started, you are racist! If you ask about alternative prevention or therapeutics, you are anti-science! Imprisoning the victims and hailing perpetrators of this plandemic... and **if you dare** to opt-out of said prescriptions, you will be refused entry into your "own" nation, schools, and businesses ...until you comply!

BTW, still trying to figure out how ***Person A*** can make ***Person B*** sick when ***Person A*** is not sick, and ***Person B*** is protected from said sickness!?!

If the gene therapy vaccine works, those who take it should be protected, but if it offers no more protection than our own immunity of 99.6% against the said sickness, then what the actual _____! IF taking a shot does not guarantee you won't be reinfected or infect others ...then apparently, it's the ***free thought*** and ***free choice disease*** that needs brain-washing treatment!

Could it be that the ones creating these diseases have a financial investment in our compliance? And is it, as Justin Trudeau said, an opportunity for a complete national financial reset? A complete transfer of wealth to globalist coffers because we obviously cannot be trusted to take our medicine when mandated by our dictators!

THE TIES THAT BLIND

I just want to know whose responsibility it is to look out for Canadians if our Government won't? When I worked in the Oilfield, they always said, "Your safety is your sole responsibility!" And I believe it applies here.

Somehow, Canadians just want to mind their own business, work, and pay taxes; everything will be fine. The Police are there to protect and keep the peace, detaining and arresting lawbreakers, but now it seems their "powers" have extended to detaining and arresting otherwise law-abiding citizens. At the whim of politicians ramping up COVID restrictions, safety is no longer your concern; what the State mandates, you are no longer required to question!

There is no dialog, no question or "evidence" to consider; you have been told, and **they will arrest and confine you to prison if you try and exercise your Constitutional Rights and Freedoms.** Last year, RCMP roadblocks stopped thousands of people on main British Columbian highways, instructing people that they could not "leave their region for non-essential travel." Every time they gave an ending date, it was merely extended! The only outcomes from the lockdown measures show that the "open" States and areas had the lowest numbers of infections and hospitalizations.

Interesting how the politicians who created Martial Law Mandates had connections to the Communist Party of China. Consider the effect these mandates had on Tourism, Small businesses, and other Industries; now consider how the influx of foreign investment, workers, and contracts will replace citizens from their own resources and futures! You will soon see that it seems the more "crooked" these politicians are, the greater value they are to the Liberal Party. Ensuring that nobody rats out the other as the traitorous scumbags that they are.

They can "break ethics laws," but we will be sent to prison if we so much as attend Church!

And if they get caught, they just get 'rotated out,' and fresh scumbags are standing in the wing, ready to be installed. (Pardon my frustration, the mountains of evidence of our Government's corruption is getting to me). I would like to give some links I found while sketching out some research on this *metastasizing cancer* within the Canadian Government. Check the examples of the Liberal Cabinet selling out Canadians...

> "Imagine if a Conservative Member of Parliament had taken $73,000 worth of payoffs from any country, really — even our

allies, like America. Let alone our enemies. John McCallum, the disgraced former Liberal cabinet minister and diplomat, is China's top man in Ottawa. He literally accepted $73,000 in free gifts from the Communist dictatorship. And those are just the ones that he disclosed."
—Ezra Levant Show, July 30, 2020
https://www.rebelnews.com/ezra_levant_show_july_30_2020

"Meet John McCallum, Beijing's Top Man In Ottawa - John McCallum, the disgraced former Liberal cabinet minister and diplomat, has been corrupted by Chinese officials. GUEST Joel Pollak "John McCallum... selling information to his clients in China" **—Ezra Levant | Audio Pod Cast,** July 30, 2020
https://rebelnews.fireside.fm/els-july-30-2020

"The Ties that Bind the Trudeau Liberals to Communist China - The Liberal Party of Canada is **inseparably linked to today's CCP,** and the foundation of most Canadian-Chinese business relationships is Power Corporation, the jewel in the crown of the Desmarais family fortune. **The Liberal Party and Power Corp are interchangeable...**" Chris George, February 19, 2021 The Niagara Independent https://niagaraindependent.ca/the-ties-that-bind-the-trudeau-liberals-to-communist-china/

"Far from isolated incidents, the Canadian government has displayed **a pathology of kowtowing to China's regime** at the expense of Canadian values and sovereignty." —Neil Campbell
www.visiontimes.com/2021/02/24/trudeau-cabinet-conspicuously-absent-on-uyghur-genocide-vote.html

"KNIGHT: Liberal ties to Communist China are hurting Canada - An analysis of the Trudeau Foundation shows how money began to rain down on the foundation once Justin Trudeau took over as leader of the Liberal Party of Canada and really blossomed once he became Prime Minister. That in itself should offend all Canadians. But it doesn't because most of the mainstream media doesn't talk about it and looks the other way." —Leo Knight
https://tnc.news/2020/10/08/knight-liberal-ties-to-communist-china/

The following link exposes the communist-rooted Liberal Party of Canada ***hive*** overwhelmingly linked to China! These ties run deep and wide within the ranks of the Liberals. I had no idea that these ties are more like tentacles of the CCP working as its extension and inseparable to the core! Even the RCMP **(in more Patriotic days)** published a report ironically called ***"Project Sidewinder"*** examining the powerful influence China commands over the ***snakes*** **in the Liberal Party of Canada**; here, I thought Justin was *just—an* exception to the *(communist)* rule, turns out he's more the prerequisite!

> "**Just the Facts: Liberal party's connections to China's communist regime** - 1997 – The **RCMP and CSIS published a joint report called Project Sidewinder**, which examined the relationships between powerful players in China and Canada,"—True North Wire, https://tnc.news/2020/04/22/just-the-facts-liberal-partys-connections-to-chinas-communist-regime/

What do the Liberals get for their passionate relationship with China? Are we to believe it is reserved to petting and foreplay? Or is our *free* nation getting screwed? Especially when plenty of taxpayers have no idea their "representatives" are *pimping* them out to anything *RED* that walks!

Justin Trudeau once said in a 2012 op-ed...

> *"From minerals to energy, from education expertise to construction, we have a lot of what China needs,"*

...but how about what Canada needs? Do we need more China-Style basic dictatorship, lockdowns, and destruction of the Canadian economy? WHO profits? It seems we are already paying China to take Canada off our hands!

It is very telling when the Trudeau Cabinet abstains from a vote declaring that China's genocidal action against more than a Million Uighurs is horrendous. If it is too much for Liberals to condemn genocide, I guess we know where we will *beheaded!*

Trudeau praises China for its basic dictatorship, so I am sure if JT could get more of China's Military training on Canadian soil at the *slavery rates* in China, he would probably use them to turn our economy ***around on a dime!***

> "Trudeau moves from China's 'useful Idiot' to something more dangerous - It's the accumulation of everything we've seen with Trudeau, his allowing China to take over sensitive Canadian national security companies, his willingness to criticize India and the United States but go easy on China, his expressed admiration for China's "basic dictatorship," and now his desire to have Chinese Communist troops on Canadian soil to learn winter warfare tactics... " —OPINION
> https://thepostmillennial.com/trudeau-moves-from-chinas-useful-idiot-to-something-more-dangerous/

DEVASTATING footage appears to show **coronavirus patients being welded inside their homes and "left to die"** as China battles to contain the fatal disease.
https://www.the-sun.com/news/378365/coronavirus-patients-welded-into-homes-in-china-as-death-toll-spirals-to-813/

"Audiobook now available! **CHINA VIRUS: How Justin Trudeau's Pro-Communist Ideology Is Putting Canadians in Danger**"
—Rebel News
https://www.rebelnews.com/china_virus_justin_trudeau_putting_canadians_in_danger

"Trudeau's B.C. Senate appointee a Beijing apologist, MP charges - B.C.'s newest member of the Senate has been accused by the Conservatives of being an "apologist" for Beijing's "unacceptable" behaviour in asserting territorial claims in the South China Sea." —Peter O'Neil
https://vancouversun.com/news/local-news/trudeaus-b-c-senate-appointee-a-beijing-apologist-mp-charges/

"**Canada supports China's ongoing response** to novel coronavirus outbreak"
News release"
—Global Affairs Canada
https://www.canada.ca/en/global-affairs/news/2020/02/canada-supports-chinas-ongoing-response-to-novel-coronavirus-outbreak.html

On a personal note, one of the first hymns I learned was "Blest be the tie that binds," authored in 1782 by John Fawcett ...a full two hundred years before I humbled myself to Christ...

Blest be the tie that binds
our hearts in Christian love;
the fellowship of kindred minds
is like to that above...

Such is not the sentiment of Marxist mandates, where each soul is forced to bear *the mark* and *global branding* of the State. Personal autonomy is lost to a governed *herd mentality*. If God-given love, freedom, and community enjoyed in Canada are in a *"Blessed tie that binds,"* ...the chaotic division of greed, hate, fear, and its disparity is definitely cursed in those ties that blind!

REFLECTION ON REFLECTION

When I was a kid, we sang O Canada and said a prayer before class in Catholic school. It wasn't some *magical mantra* that made things better, but it helped us feel that we were a part of something bigger, worth living for and dying for. One could laugh and fool around during many activities, and even as the "class clown," I don't remember making trouble during those times. In my mind, I was somehow transported to a battlefield in salute with planes overhead, under a sky our God created for our enjoyment and protection.

Not my sky but our sky, recognizing ***"the supremacy of God"*** as in the first words of our Constitution, Charter of Rights and Freedoms! Such secure beliefs and happy times; simple rules, clear goals; a life that seemed anyone could live. Back then, we were still relatively fresh from the World Wars; some in our families personally fought and survived, and many felt that loss. We would hear straight from those heroes, and I was all ears!

Like legends of historic battles, I heard one time of my uncle Joe tell us how he ended up one night in a large bomb crater with a German enemy soldier facing him but could only see him during the light flash of bombs and firing. It would seem that crater certainly wasn't big enough for both of them to make it out alive. He could see the enemy's face, as he was sure he had no place to hide. From what I can remember, he just stood there at first thinking that it was a dream, then through the next light strobe that it was for sure but hoping against hope that it wasn't real. When my uncle said he had to decide to kill or be killed, a light flashed! And the enemy was gone!

At times, the enemy can see that they, too, are only human. Sometimes the enemy can see that they are merely fighting in turf wars to take more ground for their *"Crown!"* At times, the enemy can see that those prizes are not enough and respect your place in battle; to liberate those trapped and tortured under enemy presence in a foreign land.

The enemy often has a gun to their head, forcing them to advance another's rage and attack, and if they fail, they will be counted as the enemy they are sent to eradicate. My uncle saw no difference between himself and his enemy that night; fortunately, he lived to talk about it.

> "Ours is not to question why; ours is but to do or die!"

The problem with war is the barrage of enemy fire can make it hard to get an objective view of the big picture or the overall purpose. Regardless of your perspective, it is at the mercy of those above your pay grade! It seems many battles have a similar structure of command and procedure. Leaving patriots to fend for themselves in ***virtual trenches*** or ***media craters*** in the dark while only getting a look at "the enemy" through their narrative. Manipulated by their digest of information and monitored by their keystrokes. Those light flashes are designed to pit *warriors* against fellow workers.

In the trenches of an actual battle, all you are fighting for at that moment are those who are there with you. Many soldiers feeling abandoned resigned themselves to preserving their comrades, and their comrades in similar resolve having their back. But in the world we find ourselves in today, it is hard to determine who the enemy is, based on control orders, mandates, and lockdowns by *Canadian Health* officials.

It is tough to make sense of some *mandated* things that are neither Canadian nor about health. And more about using manipulated data **to create terms of our surrender**. But the chatter in the ranks is that "they" got this! As they partner with China, that got us here in the first place.

We are their prize, their commodity, and their future turf. Sometimes the enemy can see that the spoils of war are enough and don't respect your place in battle to liberate the trapped and tortured under enemy presence in their land.

These are those times! The enemy has a gun to their head, forcing them to advance a psychopathic rage and attack by every means, even using our government against us. If they fail, they are counted as the very enemy they are sent to eradicate. We need to take a look down that barrel! A long look past our immediate interests and financial bottom line. Because what we do will determine an honorable life on our feet or a slow death on our knees!

Melodramatic? Hyperbolic? China seems to have a system that transforms average citizens into motivated soldier spies that will mindlessly advance the same system that enslaves them to merely survive.

> "They obviously want to export that to other countries." 'Trojan horse effect' He said Beijing is using a "Trojan horse" strategy to gain influence in "many parts of the world." "They penetrate the economies, they buy up everything they can, pay off everybody they can...get a chokehold on the

> economy as much as they can and then make demands for the behavior of the government," he said."
> **—Abigail Ng | Jan 13 2020 CNBC,**
> www.cnbc.com/2020/01/13/china-is-the-most-serious-threat-to-the-united-states-james-jones.html

Do you have that kind of resolve? Does your government have that kind of resolve to advance our National Security and National interests? Or objectively, do you see our Government enriching themselves while using our money and taxes to facilitate Canada's Communist Corporate hostile takeover? Is our Government standing with Allies to prevent China's Global stranglehold over supply and demand? Using the National debt to force us to comply! Even though we are in our living rooms, we are far from home!

We are far from the home we once knew, singing O Canada and praying in schools. Instead, we find ourselves in some *trench* with a keyboard and a screen, looking for allies?

More and more Canadian citizens are marching just to get their lives back, tossing off Trudeau's *basic dictatorship* and burning their blue "toilet paper" masks that are supposed to protect them and their Grandma from the *bio-bogeyman*. You would be surprised at how many are "with us" ...or at least won't stand in our way, as we let the world know what it is like behind the Canadian Communist curtain.

The virus is real, but if you consider the kind of "hazmat" suit required to stop a virus, you would immediately stop putting up chain-link fences to keep mosquitoes out of your yard!

They flattened the virus curve; now it's time to flatten the curves of suicides, unemployment, and bankruptcies! Only essential workers are allowed to work; only essential people get to go out and fly their jets around the world on holidays and meetings with Globalist conspirators. But nothing has changed; the flu comes and goes, plagues come and go; it is surprising, though, looking back, how many of them were at China's ***"careless"*** hands? And we want their pharmaceuticals? Their therapeutics and vaccines? Their tech and social credit? I say... *"Run, Forest, Run!"*

I wouldn't even be writing books had not Google shadow-banned my website blog.

That's right! I had a simple blog, content with a few thousand hits per day, and growing. Now the only way you can get to my site by the name I coined some years back is to use another search engine where it is immediately on the top of searches and first page! Try it... "inkletter" and see who is shadow-banning ***inkletter.com*** by algorithms and political pressure. For years, I let that site go, but I still pay for the hosting, and at times, I post an article, but now I prefer writing books that haven't been burned yet!

I am just one of the millions with something to say; some of those things may not be politically expedient to their redefinition of Canada, but I write, speak, and love! As a single cog in a wheel, yet all it takes is one tooth in a gear to bring the whole mess to a stop! Some people don't see their place in our nation as "soldiers," fair enough; we still need "medics" and "transports."

We can all find some way to help or let others help. Many years back, I worked for a Stucco contractor Rob; he had a saying that fits here, *"Lead, follow or get out of the way!"* Maybe, on *our way* **past the next mirror**, we should ask ourselves, "Am I a Canadian?" Good, bad, or otherwise... **Am I Canadian?**

But just in case I get the idea that I can voice my Canadian patriotism and protest in Ottawa... they have raised the gas prices so much that I must *"shelter in place"* until their planned inflation eats up all our resources. **Maybe** while I am locked down in my community by financial handcuffs and leg irons, I can reflect a bit on the unreported havoc mandatory vaccinations have had on us:

VAERS Summary for COVID-19 Vaccines through 6/3/2022
https://vaersanalysis.info/2022/06/10/vaers-summary-for-covid-19-vaccines-through-6-3-2022/

Are VAERS records for Covid-19 Vaccines being deleted every week???
https://vaersanalysis.info/2021/06/10/are-vaers-records-being-deleted-every-week/

***UPDATE on Death Record of 2-Year Old from Alaska SCRUBBED from VAERS
https://vaersanalysis.info/2022/03/05/update-on-record-of-2-year-old-from-alaska-scrubbed-from-vaers

Get Your Copy of All the VAERS Symptoms for the COVID-19 Jabs
https://vaersanalysis.info/2021/11/24/all-the-symptoms/

BUT...The Pfizer Trial Showed that the Vaccine is Safe and Effective, RIGHT?
https://vaersanalysis.info/2021/11/18/but-the-pfizer-trial-showed-that-the-vaccine-is-safe-and-effective-right/

Are there alternatives to the COVID-19 Vaccines for the treatment/prevention of SARS-CoV2?
https://vaersanalysis.info/2021/07/02/are-there-alternatives-to-the-covid-19-vaccines-for-the-treatment-prevention-of-sars-cov2/

O CHINADA

Do I think Trudeau is a traitor?

Some people think that Justin looks like his father (allegedly Fidel Castro), **I think he looks more like his mother, Margret Trudeau**, but that's just my opinion. I am more concerned with the policies of Justin Trudeau and how they may lean toward *Cuban-type communism*; because if they lent more in line with his father (Pierre Trudeau), they would be more of a *Chinese-type* communism.

Justin Trudeau touts a kind of *faux feminist* post-nationalism that sounds inclusive, but it's just code for communist globalism! And seeks to follow in goosestep with his historical communist role models that grabbed Cuban and Chinese guns from patriots before they woke up! And this Coronavirus exercise proves the kind of direction we are headed. In times past, they quarantined the sick and let the healthy be free to build a nation. Now they quarantine the healthy so that they can dismantle that same nation!

No matter what they say, it's not about *"Herd Immunity"* ...but Herd Mentality!

Here is some proof that Canadians are about to be taken over by a China or a Castro-communist event and evidence of Justin's treason...

> "Trudeau Just Sold Out Canada's National Security To China...Despite warnings against the deal from the Department of Defence and CSIS, the Liberal government has let China take control of a Canadian company with close links to our national security."
> —SPENCER FERNANDO
> https://spencerfernando.com/2017/03/28/treason-trudeau-just-sold-canadas-national-security-china/
>
> "Trudeau govt funds China biolab linked to origin of pandemic almost $1M for coronavirus research The grant, linked to the University of Alberta, will help 'team members' at the Wuhan Institute of Virology to perform tests
>
> April 16, 2020 (LifeSiteNews) – Canada's Liberal government under Prime Minister Justin Trudeau has given close to $1 million of taxpayer money to help fund "research" for new COVID-19 "screening and diagnosis" tools at the Chinese lab where the virus is suspected to have originated. The funds were granted to a researcher from the University of Alberta, who received $828,046 from the Government of Canada's $27 million coronavirus research

> fund, Rebel News first reported. This fund was announced in February and was set up to "contribute to global efforts to address **the 2019 Novel Coronavirus outbreak."** — https://www.lifesitenews.com/news/trudeau-govt-funds-china-biolab-linked-to-origin-of-pandemic-almost-1m-for-coronavirus-research

Can we trust the same people who funded the Chinese Wuhan lab and created this Global *Planedemic* with a vaccine fix? How stupid do we have to be? Many wonder why they cannot get Google search results on these topics. The answer is simple; they are shadow-banning any whistle-blower reference to this Marxist takeover of Canada. **Google is not your friend!** Even the American Government doesn't use it anymore for their *spying*!

> "**Google will stop selling its artificial intelligence expertise to the Pentagon** in a controversial partnership that saw massive pushback from the Mountain View firm's employees, according to a new report.
> The digital advertising and search giant, which holds "Do the right thing" as its motto and hauled in $110 billion in revenue last year, had sought to use "Project Maven" as a "golden opportunity" and stepping stone to lucrative military contracts, the report said." — **Ethan Baron,**

> www.military.com/daily-news/2018/06/03/google-backs-pentagon-project-after-uproar-report.html
>
> "Justin Trudeau invited China's People's Liberation Army (PLA) to send its troops for cold weather training at CFB Petawawa in Ontario — and Trudeau raged at the Canadian Armed Forces (CAF) for cancelling the training after China kidnapped Canadian citizens Michael Spavor and Michael Kovrig. This is only one of many bombshell revelations in The China Files, a 34-page access to information document released by the Trudeau government to Rebel News, seen below. Documents that normally would have been completely blacked out by government censors were instead greyed out — the documents remain completely readable. Rebel News has chosen to black out a very small portion that would otherwise compromise the safety of an individual." **Read the secret "China Files" now!** — By Ezra Levant
> https://www.rebelnews.com/the_china_files

Is that what Liberals voted for? Is that what Canadians voted for? Don't think for a maple-leaf minute that our governing class is in the dark about these things! Now that the gig is up, will we see more lockdowns to keep us from the ballot box so that we can have an *"election"* just like the one perpetrated in the United States?

If Trudeau's cabinet members aren't outraged by this info, they **ALL** are in on it!

Not to mention the RCMP —are they not there to serve and protect our nation? Where is their investigation? Where is the Canadian Military in all this? Have they swung from our Allied Forces to partner with China? O Chinada!

The following links are a must-read to be more informed about how Trudeau has opened the door to selling off Canada to China...

> "China Owns Canada...Canada was the global leader in technology. Now those billions of dollars and ultimately 100's of 1000's of high paid, highly skilled employees, along with world leading Canadian technology, now belonged to China... From the very top, our Government has been completely infiltrated by the Communist Government of China. These senior officials are either directly complicit in the motives of China, or are direct agents of the Chinese Government and Communist Party... Trudeau has sent $100's of Millions of dollars to China. Under the guise of "climate change" and "women's health"
> —Andrew Rouchotas,
> https://therealtruthnetworkcom.wordpress.com/2020/09/02/china-owns-canada/

"CBC National: CSIS director says foreign governments (China and others) infiltrating local, provincial governments... Richard Fadden reveals that CSIS has ongoing investigations into politicians at the provincial and municipal lever who are agents of influence for foreign governments in Canada." CBC National, Jun 22, 2010
https://www.youtube.com/watch?v=5j-tRKdMx8g

"CHINA OWNS CANADA: CHINESE TROOPS, BIOWEAPONS (and forced Native Vaccinations) —KEVIN ANNETT VIDEO: skip to the time marker 7:15, The Phaser | May 23, 2021
https://thephaser.com/2021/05/china-owns-canada-chinese-troops-bioweapons-kevin-annett/

"Chinese buy up Canada farms; is Beijing behind it?
OGEMA, Canada (AFP) – With too few farms in China to feed a burgeoning population, Chinese immigrants have started buying up agricultural lands in Canada and shipping produce to Asia... after Chinese state-owned firms poured vast sums into neighboring Alberta's oil sands -- many in rural Saskatchewan are quick to believe that Beijing is now targeting their farmland to feed its people." Fox News,
https://www.foxnews.com/world/chinese-buy-up-canada-farms-is-beijing-behind-it

Intelligence has never been a factor in *Justin Trudeau's Canada*; just because the USA cut ties with Google spy tech, it doesn't mean Justin Trudeau has to follow intelligence. INSTEAD, it has been uncovered that the Trudeau Government has been sharing intel with China and training the Chinese military in "**cold weather warfare**," yes, I think that **Justin Trudeau is a traitor.**

Question: are the **RCMP** being used as globalist mercenary thugs, complaisant with Trudeau's treasonous crimes, to protect him from prosecution? Maybe they are under ROYAL ASSENT and decree to perpetrate an assault on Canadian democracy? By not enforcing the law when it comes to the political ruling class and then targeting peaceful Canadians with arbitrary "mandates," they destabilize the country to necessitate more government control! And WHO would have thought there would be political prisoners held under Canadian communism?

> "**LEAKED RCMP MESSAGES: "Time for the protesters to hear our jackboots on the ground"** RCMP currently in Ottawa to assist in the crackdown on peaceful protesters allegedly brag about using brutal force in a leaked group chat."
> https://www.rebelnews.com/leaked_rcmp_messages_time_for_the_protesters_to_hear_our_jackboots_on_the_ground

In other buried news in Canada:

> "**Chinese buy up Canada farms; is Beijing behind it?** ...Sheldon Zou inspects his equipment on his farm in Ogema, Saskatchewan, on May 23, 2013. With too few farms in China to feed a burgeoning population, Chinese immigrants have started buying up agricultural lands in Canada and shipping produce to Asia."—AFP
> https://www.foxnews.com/world/chinese-buy-up-canada-farms-is-beijing-behind-it

> "**China Is Buying Up Canadian Crude Again** The usual buyers of Canadian crude are U.S. refineries, but demand has been depressed in the United States."—Irina Slav
> https://oilprice.com/Latest-Energy-News/World-News/China-Is-Buying-Up-Canadian-Crude-Again.html

> "**FUREY: The Chinese government is still allowed to buy up Canadian firms** - that's got to change ...What they don't draw attention to, and what only gets mentioned in passing towards the end of the release, is that Shandong Gold is a Chinese state-owned enterprise (SOE). It's a company that is owned by and ultimately answers to the Chinese government."
> —Anthony Furey
> https://torontosun.com/opinion/columnists/furey-the-chinese-government-is-still-allowed-to-buy-up-canadian-firms-thats-got-to-change

COLD-WEATHER FRIEND

Growing up in a community where *my kind* was the minority in school, I understood what it was like to get bullied and be a target of discrimination. Although I had more in common with a neighboring community, yet, because I lived where I did, they lumped me in with their rivals, for which they had little use. Racism and ignorance abounded on all sides. But I found some friends who accepted me and shared my "outcast" status.

Back then, I didn't feel "at home" and left my hometown by age 15 to a bigger world. After all, just because one is paranoid doesn't mean the world isn't out to get you! We all find ways of coping with the scenarios we get tossed into; mine was alcohol, drugs, and martial arts.

I was fascinated with indigenous peoples and starving for culture in a multi-cultural smorgasbord; I loved geography and history. Hearing stories of ancients, their lands, and languages,' it came as no surprise that one day I would take a couple of road trips with my family later in life, to Guatemala through the States and Mexico in a couple of buses that I restored; One bus was a *65 Schoolie*, and the other a *68 Fishbowl*.

We learned enough Spanish to get in and out of trouble, but most importantly, we got to know some of the most loving people. It seems that the less these souls had, the more generous they were! If you have poor self-esteem and want to feel loved, live and **serve** among the impoverished.

However, when I was young and being **"white as bread,"** my personal glory was that I could tan well, but no matter how I tried to look brown, my skin would always retreat to its original color(s). Like a sponge, I tried to absorb the cultures I encountered and learn a bit of their languages and phrases; my kids laughed at me around other cultures as my accent changed!

My idea of a good time is to watch foreign movies (mainly Spanish and Chinese) while reading the sub-titles; strangely, it doesn't seem right not to have the volume cranked even though I can't understand a lick! Somehow, I am hoping to learn by osmosis, yet something that is probably only a stereotypically "Hollywood" anyways.

Even though I was an angry youth, I would have never considered using my interest in cultural differences to exploit specific weaknesses and traditions to my advantage in a fight. Mine was more a knee-jerk reaction to other arguments over things that could have been more often solved by listening than yelling. But I did learn a few things:

one doesn't have to win "the battle" to "win the war!" Martial Arts is about deception and misdirection, guiding your opponent into the moves you can easily defend or exploit.

It, too, is a deception; to appear strong when you are weak is also a dead give-away! IF your opponent is predictable at any level, it is only your lack of skill and laziness that ensure your defeat. And to those who would seek to destroy you by a nonphysical verbal assault, you only can control your anger and ego for a more convenient time of engagement; unless a public demonstration of your merciless resolve is an advantage.

Time is teaching me that there is a season for peace and a season for war, and from my experience, it is better to make war from the position of defense rather than ambition. To seek advantage for mere advantage's sake is to forfeit honor, the greatest virtue in battle.

I remember an incident where I was insulted by a guy whose older brother I respected, and I wanted to let him know why I was going to pummel his younger brother out of courtesy. The older brother wasn't a mouthpiece like his younger brother, nor was he a fighter, but his response ended the confrontation. He just clenched his fists and told me (shaking) that he couldn't let me do that regardless of what happened to him.

Now that is honor!

Only a godless, heartless enemy wouldn't respect honor and why it is imperative to have integrity, principle, and a higher calling beyond our life here and now. A person who has no honor or respect for their place in this world, given by their Creator, doesn't deserve to be served and honored. Our enemy will only befriend and make allegiances to exploit weakness, steal information to compromise our security, and betray your trust...

> "SECRET MILITARY DOCUMENTS: Trudeau invited Chinese troops to train at Canadian military bases" —Ezra Levant, Rebel News
> https://www.youtube.com/watch?v=m7YuTGEb3H8
>
> *"Justin Trudeau invited China's People's Liberation Army (PLA) to send its troops for* ***cold weather training*** *at CFB Petawawa in Ontario — and Trudeau raged at the Canadian Armed Forces (CAF) for cancelling the training after China kidnapped Canadian citizens Michael Spavor and Michael Kovrig."*
> See the full documents for yourself:
> http://www.TheChinaFiles.com

Do you think Canada has the willpower and the tenacity to fight enemies as our forefathers did in two world wars? Do you believe that the youth of our day will gladly lay down their lives (or their China-made) game controllers long enough to stand against total globalist control? Do they even know what that means and what's at stake?

Do the "adults" in each Canadian home even know why Small Business is under attack in North America? Big Corp, Big Pharma, Big Tech, and Big Debt are all BIG-CHINA. We have a *BIG* fight on our hands, or we will bow our heads in shame and surrender.

> "**Debt bondage Peonage**, also known as debt slavery or bonded labour, is the pledge of a person's services as security for the repayment for a debt or other obligation, where the terms of the repayment are not clearly or reasonably stated, and the person who is holding the debt thus has some control over the laborer."—Wikipedia
> https://en.wikipedia.org/wiki/Debt_bondage

Remembering our fallen patriots and defending their sacrifice and service is not wrong. It's not xenophobic to patriotically protect our Sovereignty and National Security. It is not racist to expect our Citizens, our Police, and foreigners to respect Canadian laws, rights, and freedoms. **It is not Canadian to betray our children** with an unsustainable debt that will make them prey to Corporate Globalist interests!

Are we such a nation that will stand against the infiltration by hostile espionage from foreign and domestic enemies? Either Canadians deserve the coming shackles on our necks, or our enemies deserve the ***ass whooping*** they got coming by honorable defenders of our Nation!

> "**Justin Trudeau Goes Full Castro-Style Tyranny** ...As Trudeau made his announcement, his army of masked leftist supporters applauded the totalitarian, further adding to the dystopian scene."
> —Grant Atkinson
> https://www.westernjournal.com/justin-trudeau-goes-full-castro-style-tyranny-moves-ban-handguns-canada/

> "**The Tyranny of Trudeau**
> The truckers are teaching him an overdue lesson in the limits of government. Humans form governments not to surrender their liberty but to secure it. ... According to this understanding of government, the proper response to a tyrannical law is disobedience. An unjust law, after all, isn't a real law at all. It is an act of violence that cries out for resistance. But self-serving government officials cast such laudable resistance as a threat to the state. In truth, it is only a threat to their tyranny."
> —George Neumayr
> https://spectator.org/trudeau-tyranny-truckers/

CHANNELING CASTRO

Justin Trudeau eulogized the late Cuban dictator by saying: *"Fidel Castro was a larger-than-life leader who served his people for almost half a century."* In defending similar statements, Trudeau said, *"I know my father was very proud to call him a friend,"* which seemed to repaint an evil Marxist regime as a model for progressive politics. It was no surprise that China's Marxist brutality enamored Justin Trudeau at his core; he spoke at a fundraiser on November 8, 2013, and said he admired China's *"basic dictatorship"* because it allowed *"them turn their economy around on a dime."* These statements reveal Trudeau's own political will.

Regardless of the public polls on which man people think Justin Trudeau's father is, that is my least concern. What gets me is who or what our Prime Minister looks to for his role model!

We cannot choose our parents, but we can choose our mentors and circle of influence. We are not merely a product of our DNA or political force that weighs on us, so I can surmise that our elected officials are taking the direction for their advantage, not ours. This kind of open-eyed evil is the kind that would see every dissenting opinion crushed beneath their feet and those lives destroyed at will, as in regimes they adore.

Canada's not so ***"soft-Marxism"*** under the Liberal Party operates unashamed as a dictatorship drowning Canada in debt by its mandates and destroying every facet of the Canadian Economy and Social Service infrastructure.

Why? Why would a political puppet (I refuse to call him a leader) trash the nation he was "elected" to serve? It seems he has his eye on a prize beyond his national responsibility. He is indebted to a globalist consortium that installed him to forward their plan to amalgamate all nations into an open, borderless society beholden to a one-world order.

As political vermin, they have infested every level of North American governments and public service; make no mistake, they will succeed. Chaos is the tool of choice, and increased chaos is the vehicle to its end...

...the end of our Charter of Rights and Freedoms!

While Canada may be under ***a soft-Marxist Socialism***, it won't remain that way for very long. I venture to say by the time of this book's publication; a full-on all-out Marxist Communism will be celebrated by this weak-willed character in the Prime Minister's office. When questioned about his praise for blood-soaked dictators, Trudeau responds fondly as his mind seems to envision sunny ways of communist grandeur for his own aspirations. And most likely has been promised as much! Such morally deficient characters seem to salivate at the thought of unrestrained autocracy. **Too harsh?**

Ask yourself an unfair question: If you had to choose between being 1) forced into the Nazi gas chambers or 2) the one forcing others into those same death chambers? Which one would you choose? Now ask the same of these "elites" who care less how many people are adversely affected by lockdowns, mandates, forced compliance or employment termination, and vaccine injury...
I think you have your answer.

These Globalist puppets have a proverbial gun to their heads by those promising them a seat in the New World Order, just like the Nazi Gestapo held a gun to the heads of all subordinates... like any gang or death cult... "Kill or be killed!"

Who are our heroes? Are they the murderers, the murdered, or those who stood in the gap to prevent such atrocities? Or those who provided sanctuary to those who got persecuted at such danger to their safety? Are we content to stand by with a cell phone camera, recording the mayhem and chaos that will soon be our reality? Like those recently riding a public transit train in Philadelphia, holding up their cellphones recording the sexual assault of a woman being raped instead of calling the police?

This isn't merely a Canadian problem; it is a problem of the *"realm"* ...look at our Queen's counterpart Australia! And look at how the unmasked and unvaxed population get stigmatized as sub-human as health-defilers, branded as super-spreaders "Typhoid Marys." The disgusting, diseased, and defiled freedom-lovers that must be punished by all social, economic, and political means. That is the future choice of all who accommodate such ideology within their ranks or political affiliation.

When the populous is ignorant of history and the Constitutional safeguards that prevent the repetition of such atrocities, the reasons for the Nuremberg trials and the Nuremberg Code become crystal clear. Yet mean little to a detached generation of "Global citizens." These have long since tossed off their identity as Canadians and counted their national rights and freedoms as trash, exchanging *"O Canada"* for a *"We are the world"* globalist anthem.

This dystopial mindset openly daydreams of a chaotic, brutal zombie apocalypse where crime is legal and butchery is the only means to a brand-new world order! A Cleansing, scorching the earth of all those who resist mandates and security measures that force government dependence on each soul, forcing not only compliance but worship! It's a *Purge* ridding our society of patriots and believers who cling to ancient documents establishing moral codes and human worth.

One store owner said, ***"If you believe the government is trying to harm us, then all is lost!"*** Ya think? In what world of hypnotism is this guy living? He is completely detached because he happens to have an "essential" business.

And that is how it is. As long as we are on top of the food chain, we don't have to worry (for now) about those trying to pick the flesh from our bones! But what happens when (eventually) those positions of sustaining supply are replaced by clean, compliant, and automatic robotic citizenry? Only then will they realize the cost of their compliance! Only then will they count the price of their soul... 30 pieces of silicon! The reality of a Communist existence. The Marx of the Beast.

Do we look forward to a "judgment day" wherein all oppressed, cheated, and starving masses will receive their compensation and equity? Or do we hold such a position that causes us to cringe at the thought of our come-up-ins? Do we still have such a position in this world where our losses here and now are counted greater than our final reward? Can we be manipulated into preserving our lives here and now at the cost of our neighbor who doesn't deserve punishment as a non-complier? We can talk all day about the moral bankruptcy of our rulers while we sell out for considerably less!

Let me canoe up that river a bit. What is the cost of the loss of our "net worth?" Let's say it is a few thousand dollars; are we willing to sell out our neighbors (like the German population ultimately did) to keep that amount? So, the cost of our character is a mere few thousand dollars? Right?

While these dictators prostitute themselves for millions? What is our humanity worth? What is our price? Many heroes who stormed the beaches to liberate foreign nations from the plague of such evil ideologies did so with freedom in mind! Not theirs, but ours! And this is how we repay them? For some pittance of social-media standing? As I contemplate Remembrance Day...

Mere youth got sent to war against the same scourge that has infected our government. The same Marxist and fascist doctrines drive the weak characters holding seats of National authority; our faithful dead must sadly look on with disappointment and bewilderment. The very nations they preserved have now thrown in their lot with such depraved dictators!

Because of faith, these souls sit at a seat of honor much higher than this world can offer. Because of such moral fortitude, these men and women threw themselves into harm's way to safeguard their children's rights and freedoms. Because of such humanity, they counted their unknown neighbor's lives worth their own and worthy of protection! IT isn't patriotic; it is simply being human; and not a Darwinian animal in a death race for survival.

Which one of our heroes are we modeling?

We didn't ask to be here in this time and space, to make such indelible marks on our society, but here we are! Are we content to "get some for ourselves," taking the opportunity over another's tragedy? Will we divide the spoils with the victors over the victims? Will we "survive" at the cost of torture, pillaging, and confiscating homes of non-compliers? Will we be content to live on our knees, or will we stand on our feet in the face of the enemy of humanity? The enemy of humanity!!

I find it so near-sighted to blame our Creator for such times as when we get forced by circumstance to make such *choices*. When the unhindered autonomy created within each man and woman can even contemplate that there is even "a choice" in the face of such evil!

Everyone will die, but not everyone will live. Again, which of our ideological heroes are we exemplifying? Everyone will share the same fate of death, but not all will share the same legacy as those who fearlessly lived!

As their Creator designed them for freedom, these lived free and filled like Himself, autonomous, creative, and purposefully complete! Not content to live like an animal in survival. Content with nothing less than living and breathing for others the same kind of love one has for themselves.

Better to have early-dreamed of heroic fortitude, than to late-waken from the nightmare of cowardice!

MAGNA CARTA

Did you know that in Canada and Australia, all "Crown Land" is declared an asset of the **Queen's private estate?**

> "Though the monarch owns all Crown land in the country, ...89% of Canada's land area (8,886,356 km2) is Crown land: 41% is federal crown land and 48% is provincial crown land. The remaining 11% is privately owned.[9]." Crown land, Wikipedia
> https://en.wikipedia.org/wiki/Crown_land

Question: if the Queen has 90% *ownership* of Canada, and she is the head of state (not Trudeau), and though he makes it easy for China to take over mineral rights of it, to do special ops "cold-weather training" on it, and opening the door to "The North American World Commodity Center Canada & China Trading Center;" ...**wouldn't that be seen as a direct contract between the Queen with China?** Canada will be China's North/South American Hub; see map (repeated in chapter Manchurian Global) from **http://nacvglobal.com/**

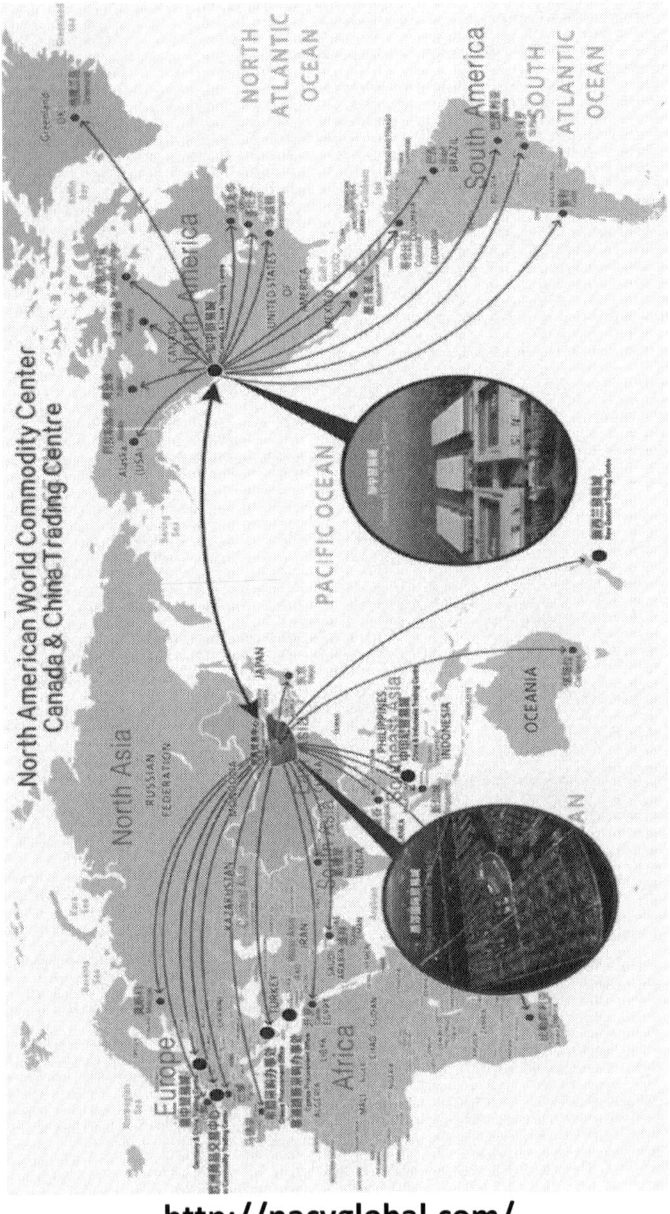

http://nacvglobal.com/

The Communist Chinese takeover of Planet Earth is happening right under our noses! Canadians are the last to know about this, **Queen-sanctioned "ambitious" venture with China in Canada!** If there is any doubt about this cooperative venture between China and our Queen, look no further than her speech at the State banquet in 2015 while hosting Xi Jinping; take note of her statement:

> *"We celebrate the ties between our two countries and prepare to take them to* ***ambitious*** *new heights."*

For the full speech by The Queen at the China State Banquet, 2015...

> "Mr. President, (Xi Jinping) Prince Philip and I are delighted to welcome you and Madame Peng to Buckingham Palace this evening. ...we celebrate the ties between our two countries and prepare to take them to ambitious new heights... Mr. President, the relationship between the United Kingdom and China is now truly a global partnership..."
>
> —Her Majesty The Queen
>
> https://platinumjubilee.royal.uk/queens-speech-china-state-banquet-20-october-2015

Queen's speech at China State Banquet
https://www.youtube.com/watch?v=gjOF_ysu8mc

OK, that actually happened. Then after a couple of years of working out some details (obviously with those two nations), **China boldly tells the world that they will soon be the World Leader!** China has the Queen's blessing and full cooperation to "celebrate the ties between our two countries and prepare to take them to ambitious new heights." It would seem pretty ambitious for these nations and United Nations **global partnership** to start addressing "pressing international challenges" from countries that don't want to get ***absorbed*** into a Globalist Marxist melting pot!

> "**China's secret plan to take over the world… or at least its "political, economic, military and environmental issues!"**
> —Joe Hildebrand, Oct. 19,
> https://www.news.com.au/finance/economy/world-economy/chinas-secret-plan-to-take-over-the-world /news-story/cd114b46e10194325422e2ef3f4eb5db

> "**China's Strategic Takeover of Canada | China Unscripted** China is playing the long game to influence and infiltrate Canada and Canadian society." —China Unscripted
> https://www.youtube.com/watch?v=arVbMBuTtss

> **REBELNEWS on CHINA…**
> https://www.rebelnews.com/tags/china?page=34

Since the Queen's endorsement of China, and their ambitious plans to take over the world, it seems there are many who want in on that opportunity coming down the pipe! From basketball players, Hollywood elites, pay-for-play politicians, and media Moguls! Why even Mark Zuckerberg wants the new "Sovereign" of the world to bless his child "by name" ...what kind of future does Mark Zuckerberg envision if he values this murderous dictator's blessing? What kind of "broken" individual would ask for such an honor from one of the world's worst? Sounds weird? These are the kinds of people who run social media entertainment and feel very liberated to fact-check your morality and mind.

> "Mark Zuckerberg asked President of China to NAME HIS BABY Ezra Levant tells the story of Mark Zuckerberg asking President Xi Jinping of China to name his unborn child." —**Ezra Levant**
> https://www.youtube.com/watch?v=xXVMpfVCfmo

> "China's President Xi Jinping 'turns down Mark Zuckerberg's request to name his unborn child' at White House dinner ...
> https://www.independent.co.uk/news/people/china-s-president-xi-jinping-turns-down-mark-zuckerberg-s-request-to-name-his-unborn-child-at-white-house-dinner-a6679156.html

Great Britain has a long-standing love/hate for the United States since America threw *"Her Majesty"* off like an *old hat* for Liberty and Independence.

And it isn't just *Ole Britannia*; no, Germany too remembers the neutering it took from America; and France... and the list goes on! America with all her "Life, Liberty and the pursuit of Happiness." The entire world runs to her borders to get a slice of that. But the Old World remembers serfdom, imperialism, and people knowing their place in ***villainage*** (legal status or condition of servitude of a villein or feudal serf); it is time for the world to recognize the real nobles and who are the villains!

"**Former CIA operative: We are in Phase 2 of a Marxist-Maoist takeover of the nation**" by WorldTribune Staff, August 26, 2020
https://www.worldtribune.com/former-cia-operative-we-are-in-phase-2-of-a-marxist-maoist-takeover-of-the-nation/

"**The Queen of England owns one-sixth of the earth's land surface**
...She is also the Queen of 32 other countries and head of a Commonwealth of 54 countries in which a quarter of the world's population lives. She is legal owner of about 6.6 billion acres of land equating to one-sixth of the earth's land surface."
—Tim's Fun Facts
https://www.timsfunfacts.com/society/the-queen-of-england-owns-one-sixth-of-the-earths-land-surface/

Now we have Germany coupled with Marxist Russia; we have "jolly ole England" coupled with Marxist China, and America taken over by Marxist Academia... **while their "Northern Neighbor" is described as a Socialist Country under Trudeau...** led by the purse by Marxist puppeteers! "The Marx of the Beast" is becoming imminent!

With the Queen of England owning one-sixth of the earth's land surface, coupled with China's unmatched Navy; and enough military to replace every man, woman, and child in North America... it shouldn't take a calculator to do the math on WHO wins and how the world can be brought to heel!

And here we thought the Queen was *weak* and merely ornamental! Knowing how ambitious both ancient nations have been and what they have done to accomplish colonization and domination in the past... just know that the Queen and *Emperor* of China are preparing to take their Globalist Partnership to "ambitious new heights!" With all the atrocities these nations have committed throughout history with their mercenaries, **one wonders** what "new" *ambitions* are to be unleashed upon an unsuspecting world? Important questions remain:

1. How is it possible in **democratic** Canada that we are born subjects to a Queen?

2. Did she pay for that 89% share of the land that **belongs** to Canada?
3. How does the Queen own anything in Canada **without** being *"Sovereign?"*
4. **Did we get a vote** to allow the Queen the right to sell off Canada to China?
5. Why isn't Canada's "Crown Lands" deemed and used as **Public Lands?**
6. Did you know that **the only Supreme Sovereign in our Constitution is God?**
7. Do you know what **Magna Carta** is and how it applies today?

The Magna Carta Libertatum *(Medieval Latin for "Great Charter of Freedoms"),* ***By declaring the sovereign subject to the rule of law*** *and documenting the liberties held by* ***"free men,"*** *the Magna Carta is the foundation of freedom against arbitrary orders of tyrannical dictatorships...*

https://en.wikipedia.org/wiki/Magna_Carta
https://www.britannica.com/topic/Magna-Carta

It is no wonder that the next King of England and *Canadian King* will replace the **Magna Carta** with a Terra Carta "Earth Charter." All **in the name of Climate Change**, to annul our Human Rights for what they will deem so-called Earth Rights. These *Earth Rights* will exchange God-given Rights for *Earth-Sovereign-given Rights.*

The very first words in our **Constitution and Charter of Rights and Freedoms** are its premise and define our identity as Canadians; we must return to our foundry!

> *"Canada is founded upon principles that recognize the* ***supremacy of God*** *and the* ***rule of law****"* **Constitution Act, 1982**

Our Constitution, the Charter of Rights and Freedoms... is our "**Magna Carta!"** The document of our Canadian Constitution declares that there is **only one Sovereign** with supremacy, and it isn't Trudeau or the Queen! **"Terra Carta"** is a means by which the **Prince of *Wales*** has declared **an end to God-given human rights**, so he alone gets to **create... "global value."** He alone will assert "Earth Rights," which will trump human rights. Assigning ***global value*** will determine who will be deemed "essential or nonessential."

> "The **'Terra Carta'** offers the basis of a recovery plan that puts Nature, People and Planet at the heart of **global value creation** – one that will harness the precious, **irreplaceable power of Nature** combined with the transformative innovation and resources of the private sector."
>
> —The Prince of Wales

***Wale, noun:** "A mark raised on the skin, as by a whip; a weal or welt."

Some say the Monarchy is merely a figurehead and not a functional Head of State; I say okay, remove the roleplaying of a Monarchy and give Canada back to her people. Let Crown Lands become Public Lands and let us return to a Canada *"founded upon principles that recognize the supremacy of God and the rule of law."*

THE PATSY

Picture yourself as **a firefighter facing a public enemy arsonist** running around lighting fires too many to count—any of which could be nationally catastrophic! Consider yourself a diligent appraiser of the situation and attempt to report all said fires by the arsonist to the authorities, only to be met with evidence that those same authorities are in cahoots with the arsonist. Furthermore, the more you try to expose the truth, the more you realize that the authorities are not in cahoots with the arsonist. Instead, they have employed him to their advantage to create chaos that they alone can provide the solution to.

This book barely scratches the surface of just one *"fire"* ...the **Marxist "penetration"** of the Government in Canada. But the more we point the finger at the ***arsonist*** **(Justin Trudeau)**, we find that **he is merely a patsy for the takeover.**

It turns out that their **conspiracy** with the oppositional NDP, Bloc Québécois, Green Party of Canada, and even the Conservative Party of Canada (that is, until the removal of Erin O'Toole from leadership); has taken **"controlled opposition"** to a new level even for banana republics! Conspiracy for what, you might ask...

an autocoup d'état!

Leaving aside the thousands of deaths and injuries from forced experimental gene therapy shots; not to mention the criminal termination of livelihoods by mandated experimental gene therapy shots; and to say nothing of **the conspiracy between the Liberal Government with China** to develop and release a bioweapon, to facilitate the very development to implement these experimental gene therapy shots (and endless boosters) ... let us move on to matters of the Law concerning Treason.

One of the biggest problems I had writing this book was that I couldn't get down on the page fast enough, the number of Liberal scandals and treasonous betrayals of Canada! Every day it seemed new reports of Trudeau **literally** trampling on the people of Canada became commonplace.

To say that Liberal Justin Trudeau is a complete failure is too nearsighted. He seems to have done even more for Marxist Globalism than Biden to treasonously destroy the nations of their birthplace! It was like a foreign communist plant was in control of our government, driving it like a run-away freight train toward a destiny of destruction!

Our Canada is a great place to live, work, and play; what amazing nature and freedoms, all paid for in blood by our forefathers, albeit willingly or conscripted. Those sacrifices built our nation, and that heritage and legacy uphold "the highest law in all of Canada" our Constitution and Charter. Our ancestors and future generations will have died in vain if we lose vision, if we lose purpose and if we lose our identity as Canadians!
If we break faith with those who died...

"**In Flanders Fields**
In Flanders fields the poppies blow
Between the crosses, row on row,
    That mark our place; and in the sky
    The larks, still bravely singing, fly
Scarce heard amid the guns below.
We are the Dead. Short days ago
We lived, felt dawn, saw sunset glow,
    Loved and were loved, and now we lie,
        In Flanders fields.
Take up our quarrel with the foe:
To you from failing hands we throw
    The torch; be yours to hold it high.
    If ye break faith with us who die
We shall not sleep, though poppies grow
        In Flanders fields."
—Canadian physician Lieutenant-Colonel John McCrae, May 3, 1915

This testimony is why *NATIONALISM* be damned.

Every *China-friendly* Hollywood movie condemns "nationalism," and each woke liberal media hack equates *nationalism* with racism; WHY? Because nationalism holds to a **nation's** law and order!

Each law defines and protects a nation's citizens; no nation, no citizen, and no protection! It is why Globalism wants to dissolve borders, not because they want to help poor dislocated peoples of the world... but rather to create a world of dislocated peoples that will be dependent on their rules, laws, and dictates! Remember the 5th point of the **World Economic Forum 'Agenda 2030'**: ***"A billion people will be displaced by climate change.*** ***We'll*** *have to do a better job at welcoming and* ***integrating refugees."***

Yes, displaced by a *SOCIAL-CLIMATE* CHANGE!

We now have a lawless Monarchy, lawless politicians, and lawless courts! **Only God is supreme!** Yet we have a Monarchy, politicians, and courts playing *god* as they dictate arbitrary mandates and *laws* destroying our nation's very fabric.

I once sat in a courtroom where a lawyer quoted a passage of the law to the Judge for his remembrance, **BIG MISTAKE!** The Judge barked...

"I AM THE LAW IN THIS COURTROOM!"

And there you have it! These authoritarians believe they are above the law, handing dictates down to us peasants of the realm! To them, we are merely subjects to be bartered and traded as merchandise of their holdings under *"The Crown."*

But our constitution protects us from such tyranny. Every Monarch, member of parliament, court, and law enforcement agent is subject to the oath and defining Constitution and the Laws that make their authority valid! Our laws protect us from this kind of dictatorship! Again, this is why they must dissolve our national identity as a constituted society of laws and order.

Do you know why the accusation of "insurrection" is now being levied against the law-abiding citizenry? **Because this is precisely what they are doing!** These are the treasonous insurrectionists destroying the foundation of Canada!

"Treason

(2) Every one commits treason who, in Canada,

- **(a) uses force or violence** for the purpose of overthrowing the government of Canada or a province;
- **(b)** without lawful authority, **communicates or makes available to an agent of a state other than Canada**, military or **scientific** information or any sketch, plan, model, article, note or document of a military or **scientific** character **that he knows or ought to know may be used by that state for a purpose prejudicial to the safety or defense of Canada**;
- **(c)** conspires with any person to commit high treason or to do anything mentioned in paragraph (a);
- **(d)** forms an intention to do anything that is high treason or that is mentioned in paragraph (a) and manifests that intention by an overt act; or
- **(e) conspires with any person to do anything mentioned in paragraph (b) or forms an intention to do anything mentioned in paragraph (b) and manifests that intention by an overt act.**"https://www.laws-lois.justice.gc.ca/eng/acts/C-46/section-46.html

Aren't arbitrary mandates of the Prime Minister for medical procedures against personal bodily autonomy an assault and crimes against humanity? Aren't arbitrary ***war measure* acts** against Canadian citizens criminal? What about public statements given by Trudeau confirming his corroboration with the **World Economic Forum (WEF) Agenda 2030 Great Reset?** Is this not openly the overthrowing of Canadian Democracy and nothing less than treason?

A couple of quotes reported on Global News revealing his public membership in the **WEF** and part in the **Great Reset 2030 Agenda**... you know, where we are all ***"own nothing, and be happy."***

> "**The elites want COVID-19 lockdowns to usher in a 'Great Reset' and that should terrify you** "TRUDEAU: This pandemic has provided an opportunity for a reset. **This is our chance to accelerate our pre-pandemic efforts** to reimagine economic systems that actually address global challenges like extreme poverty, inequality and climate change." –Tucker Carlson
> https://www.foxnews.com/opinion/tucker-carlson-coronavirus-pandemic-lockdowns-great-reset

These are **"pre-pandemic plans"** to **"maintain momentum"** in surrendering Canada to the Klaus Schwab 2030 Globalist agenda! Schwab brags that ***"we penetrate the cabinets"*** and is proud that he *owns* Trudeau and over half of his cabinet! Our political representatives have sworn an oath to uphold the constitution and be loyal to Canada; **"Trudeau and over half his cabinet" have betrayed our nation's trust!**

> Klaus Schwab, Trudeau, and other Globalist leaders penetrated Cabinets
> www.youtube.com/watch?v=RxtiD8Z6gBI&t=27s
>
> Klaus Schwab has Justin Trudeau affirm his commitment to making an **"Open Canada"** as a representative
> https://brandnewtube.com/watch/justin-trudeau-039-s-allegiance-to-klaus-schwab-amp-the-globalist-agenda_kfMzh4REgZAZ9pe.html
>
> Woman confronts Justin Trudeau: "We used to hang traitors!"
> https://www.bitchute.com/video/qLbPKUMR3spy/

Where is the Law in our land? Am I just the subject of a tyrannical realm? Or, am I **a Canadian** under the "***supremacy of God*** *and the* ***rule of law?***"

It is one thing to debate whether or not Trudeau has committed treason and another to see him held accountable. **Is it just a coincidence that Cameron Ortis (senior RCMP intelligence official) *** ***"a potential Chinese spy*** *infiltrated the highest* *levels of the Canadian intelligence service which is part of the Royal Canadian Mounted Police... was likely spying for China from at least 2015"* **...same year Trudeau **accepted donations from a Chinese gov advisor, to his father's foundation!**

> *** "China seems to have infiltrated Canada's highest intelligence agency** –and it's not the first time..."
> https://americanmilitarynews.com/2020/05/china-seems-to-have-infiltrated-canadas-highest-intelligence-agency-and-its-not-the-first-time/
>
> ** "Zhang Bin is a political advisor to the Chinese government, and **after attending the event, he and his partner ... donated $1 million** ... including $50,000 to build a statue of the former prime minister."
> https://www.cbc.ca/news/politics/chinese-fundraiser-trudeau-statue-1.3863266
>
> " In the book Red-Handed: **Peter Schweizer Exposes Canadian PM Trudeau's Deep China Ties** *'We know the prime minister's love for the Chinese dictatorship, so what exactly did he promise the Chinese for (a) million dollar donation?"*
> *https://headlineusa.com/peter-schweizer-exposes-canadian-pm-trudeaus-deep-china-ties/*

"Two Chinese defectors say the Chinese government has a network of **more than 1,000 spies and informants in Canada."** ... https://www.cbc.ca/news/canada/defectors-say-china-running-1-000-spies-in-canada-1.557085

How much is Trudeau's admiration for China's basic dictatorship costing Canadian taxpayers? ... **Canadian foreign aid to China totaled $41 million** (2019), according to newly-released data from the Department of Foreign Affairs. **China has a $13 trillion economy and $10 billion space program**." https://www.rebelnews.com/trudeau_government_41_million_foreign_aid_china_included_pollution

What is an autocoup d'état? ...just asking for 38 Million friends!

"A self-coup, also called **autocoup** ...is a form of coup d'état in which a nation's leader, having come to power through legal means, dissolves or renders powerless the national legislature and **unlawfully assumes extraordinary powers not granted under normal circumstances... assume dictatorial powers.**" https://en.wikipedia.org/wiki/Self-coup

AUTOCOUP

The sinister thing about an **Autocoup** or **Self-Coup** is that it creeps in under the guise of legality, unlike an all-out military **Coup d'état**. And it doesn't take as much effort; the treasonous greedy globalists already fill "progressive cabinets." This way, the slimy dictator comes in all "legal" and then uses the misguided "don't want to lose my job" drones to secure their stronghold. But the worst thing about these autocoups is that they serve the installers, not the actual *seat-warmers*.

The faceless powers behind these government take-overs hide in anonymity because they would be in trouble if people revolt.

The same thing happening in Canada is happening in the United States. These get into power through *legal* means and arbitrarily pass laws that render the opposition powerless. If they cannot pass laws to further their agenda, they arbitrarily take away citizens' rights by trampling them by using any means necessary. From exorbitant taxes through gas/carbon to targeting them by medical *laws* and federal mandates. Now the citizenry can fight these measures, but it takes time and money; all the while, they may sit in jails or suffer the loss of their livelihoods and freedoms!

What about the local autocoup effect in cities and towns? It gets nasty when local and city-level bureaucrats become **gatekeepers of the autocracy**, using by-laws and ordinances to stop and hold up any building and production. These get into their positions of power *legally* and then hold Cities and Towns hostage by regulations which cause inflation and property values to increase. These measures make it nearly impossible for the homeowners to fix their properties and must sell to those who will then sit on said properties or turn them over for three and four times the price.

> "A famous Supreme Court justice said that the power to tax is the power to destroy. **Similarly, the power to regulate is the power to destroy.** –Harold Demsetz, of the University of Chicago, in a speech given at the University of Winnipeg, January 1970."
> https://www.hoover.org/research/trumps-deregulatory-successes

> **Jordan Peterson, Pierre Poilievre interview**
> "We discussed his election efforts, Canada's energy infrastructure and economic policy, as well as Poilievre's mission to tackle the housing crisis, lower the cost of living, defund Canadian media, and develop Canadian natural resources." May 9, 2022
> https://www.youtube.com/watch?v=C51jWWcrFc0

> "**Corruption BC** was founded by Johnny Zakharia. The mission of Corruption BC is to investigate and expose corruption, dishonesty, self-dealing, waste, fraud, and other misconduct in both public and private institutions in order to achieve a more ethical and transparent society."
> http://corruptionbc.com/about-corruption-bc/

Locally I have seen such measures first-hand; in town, building *bylaws* used to *extort* monies from homeowners who wanted to fix their properties; such properties built in the early 1900s could never be brought up "to code." Leaving owners no option but to sell cheap to those with deeper pockets who face little or no regulatory holdup because towns want to attract those *whale* developers!

Oppressive bylaws, like medical mandates, weed out the locals; by forcing freedom-sucking measures on the public. They oppress those who will fight this kind of tyranny with science and law... mandating them out of a job, while the *more than compliant* triple vaxxed and double boosted are more than happy to take their place! Those who fill their position are often imported from a fully compliant base or get forced by poverty and self-preservation to comply.

If they keep populations fearing food shortages and

higher gas prices and threaten them with more *mandates*, they will soon line up to remove those *non-compliant* just to keep their place in society. It worked for Nazi Germany.

After this exercise is complete, who do you think will be filling all the government jobs, courts, councils, and "essential businesses?" That's right, the "don't want to lose my job" drones, the "it's nothing personal and only business" drones, and the "I just have to feed my family" drones!

After all, ***your choice*** has you out of work, without medical attention, without the ability to shop in a store or get employment to pay your bills. You can comply with 5 COVID shots, 4 booster jabs, 3 Fauci masks, 2 Rapid tests, and Trudeau's *"paper drink box water bottle sort of thing!"*

Do you see this getting better? By the time you get to plead your case in a constitution-less court, with triple vaxxed Judges, double boosted RCMP, and blue-Kevlar masked military... you can kiss your assets goodbye! This is their end-game; it's for all the marbles! **And they told you to your face: *"You will own nothing and be happy!"***

Too far-fetched? Have you heard of the recent **autocratic "WHO Pandemic Treaty?"**

"**WHO Pandemic Treaty: What It Is, Why It Matters and How to Stop It.** The World Health Organization has started drafting a global pandemic treaty on pandemic preparedness that would grant it **absolute power over global biosecurity, such as the power to implement digital identities/vaccine passports, mandatory vaccinations, travel restrictions**, standardized medical care and more... A back door to global governance"
worldfreedomalliance.org/au/news/who-pandemic-treaty-what-it-is-why-it-matters-and-how-to-stop-it/

Tucker: Biden administration is close to giving WHO power over every intimate aspect of your life "So, imagine the civil liberties abuses that you lived through during the COVID lockdowns, but permanent and administered from a foreign country... **But here's the catch.** The World Health Organization gets to define what a pandemic is, when a pandemic is in progress and how long a pandemic lasts."
https://www.foxnews.com/opinion/tucker-biden-who-power-health-policy

All the major World leaders have or will sign this Pandemic Treaty, effectively making national constitutions **null and void** in response to pandemics. **WHO** would have thought that our Western Civilization would fall under the hands of the two most inept and corrupt treasonous scumbags: Justin Trudeau and Joe Biden?

Globalist rule will happen according to scripture. Some would disagree, saying our *"leaders"* would never let that happen; **in the face of the facts that prove they already have!**

IT is worse. The USA and Canada were in league with China to develop and release COVID on the world. Anthony S. Fauci said as much just after the Queen made a partnership with China, and Trump was inaugurated. IF only these two were inept, then we would have an opportunity to escape, but these "leaders of Western Civilization" are in on the worst crimes against humanity.

> "If there's one message that I want to leave with you today based on my experience, it is that there is no question that there will be a challenge to the coming administration in the arena of infectious diseases," —Fauci

Just think about it, the UN, WHO, and Davos pawns have orchestrated murder and mayhem on a global scale that cannot be calculated. All the deaths of the disease, vaccine deaths, and injury, also the deaths of delayed medical treatment or suicide from lockdowns! Merchants of Death!

Normal humans cannot understand such evil because even in their craziest thoughts, they could not be part of anything so cruel! Mass murderers and serial killers get the death penalty or life imprisonment, but these get protected by the same "legal system" that is supposed to protect us from them! We lock up those who premeditatedly kill a single person and haul those who do so accidentally into court. These traitors should be shackled and muzzled off to The Hague, but the UN that hosts such trials is just as guilty!

> "Dr. Fauci Warned In 2017 Of 'Surprise Outbreak' During Trump Administration... "There is no question that there will be a challenge to the coming administration in the arena of infectious diseases," —Fauci
> https://www.huffpost.com/entry/fauci-warned-of-trump-pandemic-2017_n_5e8a0548c5b6e7d76c65c8a4

> "**The WEF is in Canada and is running our country!!!!** "This is premeditated and preplanned; the World Economic Forum is in Canada and is running our country! And running The Great Reset, whatever the Hell you want to call it! It is happening in Canada and is being played out." —Theo Fleury joins @TuckerCarlson to discuss Justin Trudeau going after Canadians guns."
> https://twitter.com/TheoFleury14/status/1532163024445788160?cxt=HHwWgMCioeWJq8MqAAAA

Prophesies of the Bible are "batting a thousand," ...but self-serving religious pundits, not so much!

With all the global evil evident in today's world, one might want to get closer to their Creator. My prayer is not that God would be on our side but that we are on His.

> "(The Beast) ...causes all, both small and great, rich and poor, free and bond, to receive a mark in their right hand, or in their foreheads: So that no man might buy or sell, except they that had the mark, or the name of the beast, or the number of his name." —Apostle John, Revelation 13:16-17

The "Beast" isn't Liberal, Democrat, Conservative, or Green, but this evil ideology is a **Marxist RED**. The only hope against an ideological enemy is an awakening—**a return to those things that keep such evil at bay**. We have the tools, but do we have the will? The ***ink*** is wet, and the paper is dry; how will we ***right*** the last chapter of Canada?

JUST A THOUGHT

[The following is a complete chapter from my book: GARGANTUOUS/Nephilim and the Men of Shem]

"The Bible says we won't know the hour or the day of the return of Christ; however, it does say that "**the man of sin...** will be revealed in his time" ...so could it be in our time? If I were to speculate on anything related to the coming New World Order Dictatorship that's about to engulf the earth, I would say that we may have indicators that are more than obvious by now!

I mean that just as there are many "false Christs" in the world and we could recognize them by their words and deeds... **we too can realize the "Beast" by its agenda and crimes against humanity.** There has **never** been a time like ours that could have produced such a one-world government, so how would it look? Consider this scripture:

> "Now **the beast** which I saw was like a leopard, his feet were like the feet of a bear, **and his mouth like the mouth of a lion**. The **dragon** gave him his power, his throne, and **great authority**."
>
> (Revelation 13:2)

Now consider this, has there ever been a nation in history more powerful than that of the United States of America? Is there anyone more powerful than the president of the USA? No. At this time in history, there is no one with greater authority than the President of the United States, and yet **one person** spoke, and it shut down both the USA and world economies.

One person exercised more authority than that of the most powerful man in the world. He even spoke over and against the **World Health Organization (W.H.O.)**. Not only the most powerful man in the world listened to him, but everyone in the world listened to him and shut down their commerce! If the ***Beast*** existed today, **he would be its mouthpiece!**

This man may not look like much, but his authority was unquestioned, his *prescription* alone for daily life on Planet Earth was followed. To some, he seemed weak and inconsistent, to others the voice of reason, but regardless of public opinion, his authority was recognized and obeyed.

That is right; his name is Anthony Stephen Fauci.

This same man has worked with and financed dangerous Wuhan Labs in China that caused a few world-altering pandemics! With national symbols of a serpent/dragon and bear, **China holds a monopoly on Earth's medical supplies (under a snake's symbol).** This Beast is free to release pandemics, their *cures,* and then **mandatory vaccines!**

I find it most curious that Biblical prophecy has a lot to do with names and their meanings. **ALL NAMES** *(shems)* **in the Bible** are very significant, even without those involved knowing the full ramifications! **So, consider this:**

> Cambridge Dictionary:
>
> **fauci** / noun * feminine, plural + /'fawtʃi/
> **jaws, mouth le fauci del leone lion's jaws**
> —(Translation of fauci from the GLOBAL Italian–English Dictionary © 2018 K Dictionaries Ltd)
>
> **fauci** / noun jaw [noun] (in plural)
> **the mouth (especially of an animal)**
> —(Translation of fauci from the PASSWORD Italian–English Dictionary © 2014 K Dictionaries Ltd)

It is undeniable that this single man (by his word) caused the world to lock-down their economies and "shelter in place," ...and regardless of how you judge such actions, this single man had **"great authority,"** that is indisputable.

IF not only for a short time... he was the most powerful man on the planet... the far-reaching ramifications of his mere opinions remain nothing less than indelible!

Seriously, **to get the world to follow a quarantine of the healthy and not merely the sick**, it's never done before! Not logical and not scientific! That is some kind of power and great authority!

So, my question is this, if this *"Fauci"* is the "beast's" very *"mouth of a lion,"* ...does this make us within stone's throw of the Revelation of Christ?

Maybe one thing that the 2019-2020 Coronavirus Pandemic gave the world was a peek behind the veil of deception that is about to engulf the planet...

> "So they **worshiped the dragon** who gave authority to the beast; and they **worshiped the beast**, saying, "**WHO is like the beast? WHO is able to make war with him?**" (Revelation 13:4)

As I said, just a thought!"

— ["Just a Thought" © 2020 GARGANTUOUS/Nephilim and the Men of Shem]

CONCLUSIONS

I don't even know how we got here; **it must have been while we were sleeping**. When did it become possible that politicians are above the law? They fly around in private jets as treasonous puppets of Davos, using our money against us. They are supposed to prevent monopolies and price-fixing but let Gas companies collude to set higher prices, while the Government gets more in taxation from that collaboration! They destroy our economy by destroying our oil and gas industry, not to mention the environmental costs! **The following was thirteen years ago...**

> "The Guardian has reported on new research showing that in **one year, a single large container ship** can emit cancer and asthma-causing pollutants **equivalent to that of 50 million cars**. The low grade bunker fuel used by the worlds 90,000 cargo ships contains up to 2,000 times the amount of sulfur compared to diesel fuel used in automobiles. ...**a new breed of super sized container ship which consume fuel not by the gallons, but by tons per hour**, and shipping now accounts for **90%** of global trade by volume." —**Paul** Evans
> https://newatlas.com/shipping-pollution/11526/

> "We now live in a nation where doctors destroy health, lawyers destroy justice, universities destroy knowledge, governments destroy freedom, the press destroys information, religion destroys morals, and our banks destroy the economy." —Chris Hedges

A Marxist kleptocracy voted in by Eastern Canada now tightens its grip on our throats with impunity; they strangle the very life from our bodies and tax us on air they let us gasp. If they let us breathe freely by chance, they hold a press conference and brag about how heroic they are in showing mercy. And if we complain, they come back with, "Just be damn glad you aren't living in Shanghai and get welded into your homes! It's coming!

To think that a minority government has done all this chaos and mayhem! Can you imagine if they held a majority? Even now, they arbitrarily run roughshod over our constitution, laws, and Charter of Rights and Freedoms. Only one party has a chance by policy to preserve our constitution, but the NDP will team up with the Liberals, and if that doesn't do it, the others will toss in their lot. A few years ago, the so-called conspiracy folks warned everyone of exactly what we are seeing now in our world. They were laughed at and treated with contempt.

And today, more of the same!

I mentioned the constitution. **How many Canadians have read their constitution?** Or just the first part, The Charter of Rights and Freedoms? The first time I saw The Charter was in Court, it looked pretty fancy, dolled up with calligraphy and crest, but I had no idea the reason for those founding words and statutes. I have not come by many who have read the Constitution and fewer who have read the Preamble. **What is a preamble?**

> "...the preliminary part of a document, legislation, a contract or a treaty, usually setting out **what it is all about or why it has been prepared**, specially used of an Act of Parliament where Parliament expresses the general purposes of the piece of legislation.
> https://legal-dictionary.thefreedictionary.com/preamble

Similarly, I have not known many who have read the Bible or, by having read it, understand why it was written or how it was compiled. And yet it doesn't prevent some from making commentary on it or dismissing it outright. It seems each of those documents is reserved for times of trouble when there is no other place to turn to for answers or protection. It is such a time for Canada.

> "If you know the enemy and know yourself, you need not fear the result of a hundred battles. If you know yourself but not the enemy, for every victory gained you will also suffer a defeat. If you know neither the enemy nor yourself, you will succumb in every battle." — Sun Tzu, The Art of War

Our enemy knows us, the value of those things, and the legal rights we hold in trust. Our previous generation knew the enemy and died to protect us from its tyranny, but what do we know?

> "**Know this**, if the goodman of the house had known in what time the thief would come, he would have watched, and would not have allowed his house to be broken into." — The Lord Jesus Christ

We had one job to do as citizens of Canada. For the most part, we failed to know what that was or why it would be our job. That's on us, that's on us!

"For the love of God and Country," we have two founding documents, one living and one legal. The Bible and our Constitution. They remind us what it means to be Canadian... "founded upon principles that recognize **the supremacy of God** and **the rule of law.**"

—Constitution Act, 1982

"**I don't think** God gives a damn whether He's in the constitution or not." (on the Charter Preamble) —Pierre Elliott Trudeau

"If my people, which are called by my name, shall humble themselves, and pray, and seek my face, and turn from their wicked ways; **then I will hear from heaven, and will forgive their sin, and will heal their land.**" (2 Chronicles 7:14)

—The Lord God Almighty

"Because you have kept the word of my patience, **I also will keep you from the hour of temptation, that shall come upon the entire world**, to try them that dwell on the Earth." (Revelation 3:10)

—The Lord Jesus Christ

"**...choose this day,** whom you will serve..." —Joshua 24:15

"**Behold, the nations are a drop in a bucket** and are counted as the small dust in the balance: behold, He takes up the isles as a very little thing. And Lebanon is not sufficient to burn, nor the beasts thereof sufficient for a burnt offering. All nations before Him are as nothing, and they are counted to Him as less than nothing and vanity. **To whom will you liken God?**" (Isaiah 40:15-18)—The Lord God Almighty

> "All things were made by (Jesus), and without Him was not anything made that was made... **He was in the world, and the world was made by Him, and the world knew Him not**." —John 1:3, 10

> "**For by (Jesus) were all things created**, that are in heaven, and that are in earth, visible and invisible, whether they be thrones, or dominions, or principalities, or powers: all things were created by Him, and for Him:"
> —Colossians 1:16

> "Shall God not avenge His own elect, which cry out day and night unto Him, though He bears long with them? I tell you that He will avenge them speedily. Nevertheless, **when the Son of Man comes, will He find faith on the earth?**" —Lord Jesus Christ, Luke 18:7-8

> "When great forces are on the move in the world, we learn we are spirits–not animals." And he said, "There is something going on in time and space, and beyond time and space, which, whether we like it or not, spells duty." —Ronald Reagan
> https://www.youtube.com/watch?v=wpVvgNs8tqI

A thousand books cannot contain all the evil that is conspired against our Canada—neither can a thousand books contain the testimony of those who are giving and would give all to defend her.

You are not a victim; you are brought to this very moment because you are made for it! Call it destiny, call it fate, call it whatever you want but don't *'call it'* on account of rain! This storm is your opportunity, dig in and find some way to shine!

> "Hasn't God shown you what is good and what the LORD requires of you; but to do justly, love mercy, and walk humbly with your God?" —Micah 6:8

> "...he said someday I hope you get the chance to live like you were dyin'..."
> —Tim McGraw

> "Expert Panel sharing how our military is being decimated by the COVID 19 jabs! **MUST WATCH!**" —Dr. Meri Crouley
> https://rumble.com/v191xoo-expert-panel-sharing-how-our-military-is-being-decimated-by-the-covid-19-ja.html

Final questions: If there is widespread injury and death associated with these mandated vaccines, what would the purpose be to mandate them for federal employees? **Wouldn't that be the crippling and decimation of the government, military, and civil authority?** Not to mention all those who rely on travel for business! What a vacuum Globalists can walk into when their **Agenda 2030** is complete.

Well, Canadian, now is your chance! ***"Live like you are dyin'"*** **...because you are!** Should'a could'a would'a isn't going to cut it after your liberties to do those things, or anything is gone. This is just one book with one look; I pray it finds you open, readable, fitting, and timely this Canada Day;

> *"God keep our land glorious and free! O Canada! We stand on guard for____."*

Manufactured by Amazon.ca
Bolton, ON

33732492R00136